WIT

Driving across Missouri

Driving acros

Missouri

A Guide to I-70

TED T. CABLE & LUANN M. CADDEN

University Press of Kansas

Published by the University Press of Kansas
(Lawrence, Kansas 66045), which was organized
by the Kansas Board of Regents and is operated
and funded by Emporia State University,
Fort Hays State University, Kansas State University,
Pittsburg State University, the University of Kansas,
and Wichita State University

Library of Congress Cataloging-in-Publication Data

Cable, Ted T.
    Driving across Missouri : a guide to I-70 / Ted T. Cable
& LuAnn M. Cadden.
        p.   cm.
    Includes bibliographical references and index.
    ISBN 978-0-7006-1697-8 (paper : alk. paper)
    1. Missouri—Guidebooks. 2. Interstate 70—
Guidebooks. 3. Missouri—History, Local. 4. Automobile
travel—Missouri—Guidebooks. I. Cadden, LuAnn M.
II. Title.
    F464.3.C33 2010
    917.78´0444—dc22   2009044745

British Library Cataloguing-in-Publication Data is
available.

Printed in the United States of America

10 9 8 7 6 5 4 3 2 1

The paper used in this publication is recycled and
contains 30 percent postconsumer waste. It is acid free
and meets the minimum requirements of the American
National Standard for Permanence of Paper for Printed
Library Materials Z39.48-1992.

This book is dedicated to our parents,
Ted and Beverly Cable
and
Mike and Mary Lou Aiello,
who on family vacations instilled in us
the love of traveling across America by car.

Contents

Preface

Welcome to Missouri—the Show Me State. The purpose of this book is to show *you* fascinating things as you drive along the 251 miles of Interstate 70 between Kansas City and St. Louis. There is an entire genre of books on the backroads and byroads across America—guides to traveling through small towns at a leisurely pace to learn about the history, the people, and the land of those regions. But why should travelers who take the slower-paced backroads have all the fun? What about the commuters who must travel the same speedy interstate every day on their way to work or the vacationers who find the interstate a more direct route for their family trip?

We hope to slow things down a bit for you on fast-paced I-70 so that you, through our stories, may enjoy the history, the people, and the landscape, while at the same time speed up a long trip by filling your time with stories that interpret the spirit of Missouri. We hope to give daily commuters new eyes to see the land they pass by every day. And we hope to expand your peripheral vision so that as you look around, beyond the billboards, you will see the real land of Missouri. As Marcel Proust wrote, "The real voyage of discovery lies not in seeking new lands, but in seeing with new eyes."

The authors would like to thank the following individuals for reading and reviewing the draft manuscript and providing helpful suggestions for improving it: Rebecca Anderson, Kelley Blankley, Robin Grumm, Soren Larsen, and an anonymous reviewer. Wayne A. Maley, coauthor of *Driving across Kansas: A Guide to I-70*, provided much of the information found in the farm and crop-related stories. We also would like to thank the following individuals and organizations for their help in providing photographs and the Missouri trails map: Shad Aiello, Jocelyn Baynes, Keith Blankley, Kathy Borgman (Friends of Arrow Rock), Shelly Cox, Michael Dickey (Arrow Rock State Historic Site), Janae Fuller (Battle of Lexington State Historic Site), Missouri Valley Special Collections, Kansas City (Missouri) Public Library, James Harlan (University of Missouri), Marilyn Lanning (Missouri Meerschaum Company), Soren Larsen (University of Missouri), Jason Miller (Missouri Department of Conservation), Marjorie Miller (Montgomery County Historical Society), and Cliff White (Missouri Department of Conservation).

Ted Cable would like to thank his wife Diane for her encouragement and support of his passion for writing and travel. LuAnn Cadden would like to thank her husband, Mike, who calmly and honestly responded to the question, "Does this sound okay?" innumerable times over the last two years and to her daughters, Rose and Lillian, for their comic relief and understanding when Mommy needed to nurture the sometimes colicky "I-70 baby."

Introduction

The name "Missouri" comes from the corruption of the word "Oumessourit," which was the name of a nation of about 5,000 Native Americans who lived on bluffs along what is now called the Missouri River. The Peoria, an Illinois tribe of Native Americans, actually coined the name of these bluff dwellers. It meant "people of the big canoes," referring to the thirty-foot canoes that these people used to travel up and down the Missouri River.

In some indigenous languages without a traditional word for automobile, cultures created a word that literally means "canoe with wheels." In this sense, even if you are not a native of Missouri, if you are driving a large RV or truck you are truly an Oumessourit—a person of the large canoe.

Why is Missouri called the "Show Me State"? According to the Secretary of State's office website, most sources attribute the phrase to Missouri's Congressman Willard Duncan Vandiver, who served in the U.S. House of Representatives from 1897 to 1903. In 1899, Vandiver gave a speech at a naval banquet in Philadelphia in which he declared, "I come from a state that raises corn and cotton and cockleburs and Democrats, and frothy eloquence neither convinces nor satisfies me. I am from Missouri. You have got to show me."

We will avoid "frothy eloquence" as we show you the beauty of Missouri's natural landscapes and reveal ways in which Missourians have changed the landscape to benefit themselves and the world. We will show you lands of Native Americans, explored by the French, settled by Germans, and violently and valiantly fought over during the Civil War. You will drive along routes traveled by Daniel Boone, Lewis and Clark, and thousands of settlers seeking a new life in the west.

We will show you many rivers. As you enter Missouri from either the east or the west you will immediately see evidence of Missouri's tourism slogan, "Where Rivers Run." You will see two of the largest and most significant rivers in the world and cross many of their tributaries. Perhaps as you observe these many and mighty rivers and read stories about their profound impact on history and humans you will come to the realization that, as John Muir said, "The rivers flow not past, but through us."

Streams of stories also run across Missouri. We will tell the stories of early travelers who crossed Missouri and those who ended their journeys along what is now the I-70 corridor. Along the way you may even see corn, cotton, cockleburs, and descendants of those Democrats mentioned by Vandiver.

You will notice the "Show Me" slogan on the license plates of the Missouri cars that you pass along the highway. When you see it we hope it reminds you of the stalwart, inquisitive, and skeptical character of Missourians. And we trust that this book will be an excellent traveling companion and cause you to say, "Show me more of Missouri."

USING THIS BOOK

Throughout most of the route across Missouri the stories are linked to the mile markers visible along the roadside. For your driving safety, within the city limits of Kansas City and St. Louis, rather than providing stories linked to mile markers (often not visible), things to look for are presented in the order that you will see them with the mile location given parenthetically.

Note: Mile markers give the distance to the Missouri-Kansas border. Therefore, the numbers on the mile markers decrease as you head west. The distance is provided at every 0.2 of a mile. This might lead to confusion, as the stories for each mile will be started at mile markers with zero-tenths. For example, you will see markers for 150.8, 150.6, 150.4, and 150.2 before getting to the story at mile 150.0.

Missouri State Symbols

Along I-70 look for these official Missouri state symbols.

STATE BIRD

Eastern bluebirds are shaped like robins, but a bit smaller. They have a rusty breast and blue back. Look for bluebird nesting boxes on the perimeter fence at I-70 rest areas, including the ones at 58W and 166E. Nesting boxes such as these have helped the gentle bluebird rebound from population decreases due to more aggressive nonnative birds taking their natural nesting cavities. The bluebird's blue back inspired Thoreau to write, "The bluebird carries the sky on its back," and he also compared them to "a speck of clear blue sky seen near the end of a storm, reminding us of ethereal regions and a heaven which we had forgotten." Their reddish breast seems to evoke the warm summer earth. Thoreau watched as these "azure flakes" settled on fence posts. You also might see these azure flakes along highway fences or in rest areas along I-70. In 2009, S&K Manufacturing of O'Fallon donated sixty-four bluebird houses to attract bluebirds to Missouri's nineteen highway rest stops.

Eastern bluebird (Missouri Department of Conservation)

STATE TREE

The flowering dogwood dots open woodlands with white blossoms in April and May. Although this small tree (up to 40 feet) is predominantly found in the southern half of the state, you might see it mingled with larger trees along the margins of heavily wooded areas such as miles 90, 152, and 168. The four beautiful white "petals" that you see on dogwoods are actually leaves, or bracts, that surround tiny greenish white flowers in the middle. Ada Darby wrote, "The dogwood spreads white meshes—so white and light and high—to catch the drifting sunlight—out of the cobalt sky." The dogwood starts the spring in fresh green leaves and ends the season colored in deep shades of purple. Squirrels, turkeys, and cardinals are just some of the birds and wildlife that eat the tree's small oval fruits. Native Americans used the roots to make a scarlet dye and the tough, splinter-free wood of this tree was used for skewers to cook meat. The old English word *dag*, meaning skewer, translated into dogwood, which in turn gave rise to the iconic joke of foresters that you can identify dogwood by its bark.

Flowering dogwood (Missouri Department of Conservation)

STATE FLOWER

The blossom of the hawthorn tree is Missouri's official floral emblem. Because the official state flower is found on a tree, people often can't remember if hawthorn is the state tree or state flower. Although in 1923 the General Assembly of Missouri didn't specify which of the hundreds of varieties of hawthorn would be the floral emblem, the Missouri Department of Conservation attests that it is most likely the downy hawthorn. Clusters of fragrant white blossoms cover the small tree (up to 30 feet tall) in April and May and turn into tiny apple-like fruits. Birds eat these fruits and then spread the seed in pastures and along fence lines and beneath telephone and power lines, sometimes forming a hedge. In fact, the word "haw" comes from the Anglo-Saxon word for hedge or fence, and thorny varieties of hawthorn have been used as fences for centuries in Europe. Hawthorns are in the rose family and can be found throughout the state. Depending on the season you might see the clusters of white flowers or small apple fruits at any location along I-70. Missouri is not alone in this confusing designation as six other states have trees as their state floral emblem.

Hawthorn blossom (Missouri Department of Conservation)

STATE ANIMAL

The Missouri mule was named the state animal for its incredible role in Missouri's history, agriculture, mining, and even world trade as it allowed enough cotton and tobacco to be grown and shipped overseas. This strong and hardy animal ate less than a horse and yet was strong enough to pull stumps out of fields and to pull a plow through rocky ground. Missouri was the nation's leading mule producer throughout most of the nineteenth century. A mule is the offspring of a female horse (mare) and a male donkey (jack). The horse gives the mule its large muscles while the donkey gives the mule small feet that help him maneuver in rough terrain. While mules have the reputation of being stubborn, it is actually their instinct that keeps them from moving into a situation too quickly. This attribute keeps them from startling as easy as a horse. Missouri's mules passed along the Santa Fe Trail (107W). Mules quickly replaced horses as the four-legged locomotives connecting trade with Missouri and Mexico. They donned gas masks with the soldiers in World War I where the number of mules outnumbered the mechanized vehicles in the army. Over 100,000 mules assisted British soldiers in the war. At one time over 12,000 mules assisted miners in Missouri. Missouri mules were sent all over the United States (153W). They were the strong and steadfast engines that enabled the farmer to plow his fields and plant his crops, perhaps some of the same cropland that you will pass by today. Because of their history and utility, mules are the mascot for the College of Veterinary Medicine at the University of Missouri.

Missouri mule (Kansas City Public Library, MO)

STATE FOSSIL

Crinoids are Missouri's official state fossil. Crinoids, also known as "sea lilies" or "feather-stars," are marine animals that still exist in oceans, although they were more abundant in ancient seas. They are in the same family as starfish and sand dollars, but most of these creatures look more like plants with parts that resemble flowers, roots, and stems. The appearance of the fossil will vary depending on which part of the animal was fossilized. Most look like a small cylindrical piece with a hole in the middle—somewhat like a straw. These are the fossilized stalks of a crinoid. Crinoids are some of the oldest fossils on earth and were common in warm shallow seas that once covered Missouri. Today living crinoids usually are found in water deeper than 200 meters. Crinoid fossils can be found in many rock cuts along I-70, such as the ones at 77W and 76E.

Crinoid (Jason Miller)

THE MISSOURI STATE FLAG

At the rest areas ahead along I-70, you will see Missouri's state flag flying proudly. For nearly a century, Missouri did not have an official flag. Finally, in 1913, a flag designed by Marie Elizabeth Oliver was named the official state flag of Missouri. Look closely at the many intricate details and symbols. Having the Missouri coat-of-arms in the center of the red, white, and blue colors represents Missouri being near the center of the nation, and in harmony with it. Twenty-four stars around the coat-of-arms represent Missouri's position as the 24th state admitted to the Union. Missouri's Great Seal shows by its helmet and buckled belt that Missouri wants to be free to handle its own problems and indicates the power of the people. The grizzly bears signify the size and strength of the state and the courage of Missourians. The new crescent moon reminds us that we can make our future better. It is also a special heraldic symbol pointing out that Missouri was the second state formed out of the Louisiana Purchase. Can you find two mottoes on the flag? "United We Stand, Divided We Fall" encourages support for the whole United States and "Salus populi suprema lex esto" means "Let the welfare of the people be the supreme law," reminding us that state government should help better our lives.

Missouri state flag (LuAnn Cadden)

Driving across Missouri

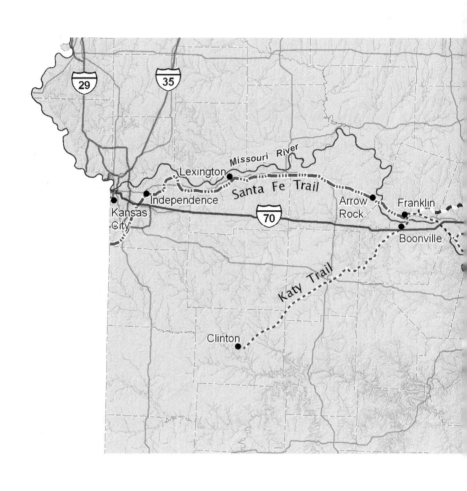

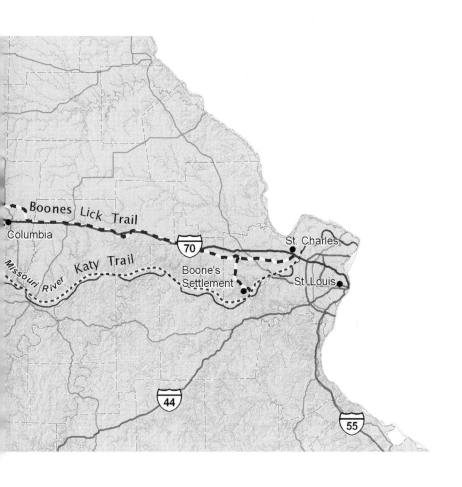

Boones Lick Trail

Columbia

Missouri River   Katy Trail

70

Boone's
Settlement

St. Charles

St. Louis

44

55

Westbound

COMING FROM ILLINOIS

"Can you see it yet?" This is the question travelers often ask when approaching Missouri. Passengers diligently scan the sky for the tallest man-made monument in the United States—anxious to be the first one to yell out, "I see it!" The "it" refers to the silver Gateway Arch, a monument twice as tall as the Statue of Liberty. You will see this first sign of Missouri near mile 11 on I-70 in Illinois. Rising 630 feet over the Mississippi, the Gateway Arch inspires awe every time you enter the city.

Made from 886 tons of stainless steel, the Arch is part of the Jefferson National Expansion Memorial. Since 1967, the Arch has soared in celebration of explorers, fur traders, pioneers, and westward travelers such as you! To some it means home, while to others it symbolizes the romanticism of the westward expansion of the United States. Visitors can enter the self-leveling elevator and take the four-minute ride to the top of the Arch to experience the 30-mile panoramic view. When looking out at the city from the top of the Arch, it is apparent that centrally located St. Louis is a nexus of transportation. Situated near the site where the two longest rivers in North America meet, St. Louis is not only a gateway to the West but also a central location where transportation systems intersect as they move people and freight across the country. Towboats push barges of grain and goods through the brown waters of the Mississippi; trains carry freight across several bridges spanning the river; pedestrians, bikes, and cars pass over the river on other bridges; and planes descend to Lambert Field northwest of downtown. The energy that makes this city run comes from power plants also visible from the top of the Arch. Power plants require enormous amounts of water, so they hug the banks of major lakes and rivers. The stacks of the Ashley Street Power Plant can be

St. Louis skyline (Shad Aiello)

seen along the Missouri shore to the north of the Arch. It originally provided power to the 1904 World's Fair. Today it supplies
the steam loop that heats the downtown office buildings.

Exit immediately after crossing the river on Memorial Drive
to join the four million people that visit the Arch each year. Below the Arch, underground, is the Museum of Westward Expansion that features exhibits about nineteenth-century residents
and travelers. Across I-70 to the west is the Old Courthouse with
its majestic green dome, where during the pre–Civil War era
more slaves sued for freedom than in any other state.

In 1764, founders Pierre Laclede and Auguste Chouteau saw
the potential of this strategic area and established a settlement
and trading post on the site. Laclede named it after Louis IX, a
French king of the thirteenth century who achieved sainthood.
Laclede said that because of St. Louis's "locality and central
position" it "might become hereafter one of the finest cities in
America." At the north end of the Arch's grounds you will get
a small glimpse on the right of the gas lamps and cobblestone
streets of Laclede's Landing. This is the area where the city began. The nineteenth-century warehouses in these nine blocks

are built with bricks made from local clay deposits. These buildings survived amid the highways and twentieth-century construction and have been converted into trendy restaurants, clubs, and shops that will take you back in time to St. Louis's old neighborhoods. From this landing, many canoes and flatboats left in pursuit of beaver pelts, gold, and land. This is also where the first steamboat, the *Zebulon M. Pike,* traveled up to St. Louis in 1817. Up to fifty steamboats could dock along these banks in the heyday of steamboat travel in the mid-1800s.

Like all rivers with towns on their banks, the Mississippi has dictated the story of St. Louis and shaped the lives of her inhabitants. And, in spite of human efforts to tame the mighty Mississippi, recent floods remind us that the river still exerts her influence over the region and its people. Poet T. S. Eliot, a native of St. Louis, wrote of this river as a "strong brown god":

I do not know much about gods; but I think that the river
Is a strong brown god—sullen, untamed and intractable,
Patient to some degree, . . .
Keeping his seasons and rages, destroyer, reminder
Of what men choose to forget. Unhonoured, unpropitiated
By worshippers of the machine, but waiting, watching and
waiting.

St. Louis's rich history includes tales of pioneers preparing to seek homes out West and immigrants finding a home here in this city. St. Louis's population exploded during the nineteenth century. It quadrupled in size between 1810 and 1840 and continued growing until it reached a peak at 857,000 people around 1950 when it was the eighth-largest city in the nation. Settlers from Kentucky, Tennessee, and other states ventured out west to escape crowded eastern cities. Many outfitted their wagons for adventure, perhaps as you would today. Others found their fortunes right here on the edge of the frontier. Immigrants from Ireland, England, and Germany came to St. Louis to find a better life and were followed by Italians, Czechs, and others. Today, St. Louis has 347,000 people—nearly the same number that lived in this city within a decade after the Civil War—making it the second-largest city in Missouri behind Kansas City. However, this figure is a bit misleading due to St. Louis's restrictive city limits (only 61 square miles compared to 311 square miles for Kansas City); in fact, over 2.8 million people live in the St. Louis metropolitan area, almost a million more than live in the Kansas City metro area.

WELCOME TO ST. LOUIS, THE GATEWAY CITY

While crossing the Mississippi, look upriver to your right to see the Eads Bridge. This National Historic Landmark is the oldest remaining bridge across the Mississippi River. When ferries were the only way of transporting freight across the river, railroad financiers in St. Louis raced to complete the bridge's construction in a rivalry against Chicago for the lead in railroad commerce. Self-taught engineer and ironclad boat builder James B. Eads used innovative construction techniques, including many firsts, to design St. Louis's first rail bridge. Eads did not give up, despite suffering a nervous breakdown while confronting many doubters and unprecedented engineering challenges. The double-deck, three-span bridge opened on July 4, 1874. It carried trains for a hundred years until it was closed in 1974. Today the lower deck is used for the light-rail MetroLink commuter trains. The upper deck was reopened for vehicular and pedestrian traffic on July 4, 2003.

While you are still driving on the bridge, directly ahead you can see the new Busch Stadium, home of the St. Louis Cardinals. You will soon be driving a 6-mile stretch of I-70 that honors Cardinal slugger Mark McGwire for his record-breaking seventieth home run in 1998. Designating a stretch of I-70 for hitting seventy home runs seemed most appropriate in 1999, but today some local politicians and fans want to remove this designation because of McGwire's link to baseball's steroid controversy. In Kansas City, you will see Kauffman Stadium, the home of the Kansas City Royals, and you will travel on the George Brett Super Highway honoring the Royals's hall of famer. When the two teams played in the 1985 World Series it was called the "I-70 World Series."

Immediately after crossing the river and curving into the

Steamboats near Eads Bridge, 1909 (Kansas City Public Library, MO)

city, to the right you can see the Old Cathedral with its gold cross, balanced high on a gold ball atop the green steeple. The cathedral has survived turbulent changes in St. Louis's history. Built in 1834 on the same site as St. Louis's first Catholic church built in 1770, it is one of the few buildings to survive the Great Fire of 1849 and was the only building left standing after forty blocks were torn down for the grounds of the Jefferson National Expansion Memorial. As you travel through the city you'll notice other beautiful old churches that once were the hearts of ethnic neighborhoods.

On the right will be the aforementioned historic Laclede's Landing area and the Ashley Street Power Plant. On your left you'll see the Edward Jones Dome. Completed in 1995, it covers fourteen acres of what was once a neighborhood of European immigrants. Up to 66,000 fans can fill the stadium to see the St. Louis Rams play football. The 12.5-acre roof weighs more than 10 million pounds. The stadium contains enough concrete to make a 47-inch-wide sidewalk from St. Louis to Kansas City. In 1999 the dome was the site of the largest indoor gathering ever held in the United States—a mass celebrated by Pope John Paul II.

Just past Exit 249, look quickly to the left to see the red-brick Polish National Church of Saints Cyril and Methodius. Built in 1857–58, it resembles churches constructed in the Lombardy region of Italy during medieval times. This Romanesque Revival style was popular with Protestants in the 1850s who desired to worship in less ostentatious buildings than Gothic- or Greek-style churches. After its Presbyterian congregation moved west,

*Michael the Archangel on Most
Holy Trinity Catholic Church
(Shad Aiello)*

in 1908 it became the first Polish National Church west of the Mississippi. This denomination had broken away from the Roman Catholic Church in 1897. They strongly supported American-style democracy, sponsoring Fourth of July celebrations and encouraging their members to become U.S. citizens. Until the 1960s, Sunday school teachers here taught not only Bible stories but also the Polish language.

Ahead on your left, you'll see the two 215-foot-tall Bedford limestone spires of the Most Holy Trinity Catholic Church. In 1849, the new German Catholic parish of Most Holy Trinity received the little church they requested for their Bremen community. Fifty years later, this impressive Gothic-style church, which can seat nearly a thousand people, was built to support the growing parish. A statue of Michael the Archangel on the south side of the church remains broken from a tornado that damaged the church in 1927. The church was repaired, but the angel was not. A story goes that the pastor would not fix the statue because the angel did not protect the parish from the damaging storm.

Just past the church, on the left in the distance, you will see a tall brick tower (247.5) and a white Corinthian-style pillar (247.4). The white pillar is the Grand water tower, built in 1871 to regulate the water from the city's first waterworks. The

Bissell water tower

younger brick Bissell water tower was built in 1886. Both towers were put out of service in 1912. These neighborhood landmarks are two of only seven historic water towers left in the United States.

The trees and lawn on the hill to the left (246.6) are part of the 127-acre O'Fallon Park, formerly the estate of John O'Fallon. Col. John O'Fallon came to St. Louis after being wounded in the Battle of Tippecanoe in the War of 1812. He worked for his uncle William Clark of Lewis and Clark fame and built a fifty-room mansion on top of one of the Native American ceremonial mounds that gave St. Louis the nickname of "Mound City."

Looking straight ahead (246.4) and then to the right as the road curves you can glimpse parts of the Bellefontaine Cemetery. Bellefontaine includes the graves of explorer William Clark; James Eads, builder of the famous bridge; Beat Generation writer William S. Burroughs; brewing magnate Adolphus Busch; Pulitzer Prize–winning poet Sara Teasdale; James Smith McDonnell, founder of McDonnell Douglas aviation company; and Thomas Hart Benton, the first senator from Missouri, who was a fervent supporter of westward expansion. Benton also survived a fight with Andrew Jackson during which he shot

Jackson and broke Jackson's sword over his knee. Jackson went on to become president and have a Missouri county named after him. You will pass through Jackson County at the end of your westward journey through Missouri. Calvary Cemetery, a Catholic cemetery, is adjacent to Bellefontaine and is home to the graves of René Auguste Chouteau, fur trader and cofounder of St. Louis; Dred Scott, a slave who unsuccessfully sued for his freedom in a famous Supreme Court case; Civil War General William Sherman; author Kate Chopin; and playwright Tennessee Williams.

Read about the ADM grain elevators on the right in the Eastbound St. Louis section (pages 147–148).

On the left at 244.2 is ABB Inc. This plant produces seventy custom-made transformers each year as well as repairing other transformers. The people who work here are in the business of "keeping the lights on." Transformers only last about forty years, and the transformers in America's fleet are on the average more than thirty years old. When you hear of "blackouts" or "brownouts" it is often because of transformer problems in the energy grid. The ABB company supplies transformers to all of the major utility companies in North America. ABB operates in 100 countries. The company is the world's largest manufacturer of electric motors and has been involved in many industrial firsts over the past 120 years. Among ABB's accomplishments, it was the first company to transmit high-voltage AC power, the first to use a combustion gas turbine for generating electricity, the first to manufacture synthetic diamonds, and one of the first to invent industrial robots.

The MetroLink tracks appear on the left near mile 239 and then cross over I-70 (238.8) and run along the right side of I-70 to Lambert Airport. Opened in 1993, this is the only light-rail system in Missouri. It makes six trips per hour traveling at 55 mph. The MetroLink benefits I-70 travelers, like you. The trains can carry 1,800 passengers per hour in a single direction, which means about 1,600 fewer cars per hour are on the highway. Almost 22 million people use the MetroLink each year. You can travel MetroLink for 46 miles from Lambert–St. Louis International Airport, just ahead on the right, all the way into Illinois.

St. Louis has been called the "City of Flight." In 2007, more than 15 million people passed through Lambert–St. Louis International Airport. Air travel has a long history in St. Louis. Long before the Civil War, balloon pilots offered flights over the city. In 1911 an aviator enthralled crowds as he flew a seaplane up and down the river going under and over the Eads, Merchants, and McKinley bridges. In 1928, Lambert became the first municipally owned airport in the country. Many important aviation firsts happened at this site. Maj. Albert Lambert, whose first flight was with Orville Wright, opened a balloon launch station here in 1920. Other notable firsts here include the first experimental parachute jump in the world and the first airplane flight of a president (Theodore Roosevelt). The first nonstop solo flight across the Atlantic Ocean began here when Charles Lindbergh climbed into his *Spirit of St. Louis* and flew to New York to begin his historic journey. The McDonnell Aircraft Company was founded here in 1939 and contributed more firsts for the United States by sending humans into space on spacecrafts designed here. The Mercury spacecraft, built here, opened up new worlds on May 5, 1961, when it launched into space the first American, Alan Shepard. Less than a year later, another Mercury capsule, piloted by John Glenn, made the first orbit around the Earth.

In 1967, McDonnell Aircraft Corporation and Douglas Aircraft Company merged to form McDonnell Douglas, which manufactured military planes such as F-15 and F-18 Hornet fighter jets. If you have been a frequent flier you have probably flown on McDonnell Douglas DC-9s, DC-10s, or their MD-80 series of planes. For thirty years McDonnell Douglas was headquartered here, until it merged with the Boeing Company in 1997. Today, this site is the headquarters of Boeing's Integrated Defense Systems, where space and military defense systems are continually evolving. The large white buildings north of Lambert's runways are part of the Boeing complex.

As you depart St. Louis County we'll leave you with some other firsts. Ice cream cones made their first appearance at the 1904 St. Louis World's Fair. And other inventions, though not invented specifically for the fair, were first introduced there: hot dogs in a bun, cotton candy (originally called "fairy floss"), and iced tea. We hope that on your journey west you too will experience some enjoyable firsts.

FROM ST. LOUIS TO COLUMBIA

The junction of I-70 and I-270 is the busiest highway intersection in Missouri. Once you successfully negotiate this intersection and return to our guide, please note that we will now begin to use mile markers to place our stories. But for those readers who are using this book in your car, we remind you that drivers should keep their eyes on the road. On average, 75,508 vehicles, including almost 13,000 trucks, drive along I-70 in Missouri each day. With this high volume of traffic caution is necessary to avoid an unwanted meeting with your fellow I-70 travelers.

234.0 Down to Earth City

Exit 231 takes you to Earth City. The strange name comes from the fact that development started in 1971, shortly after the first Earth Day. The original plan for what is now known as the "Earth City Business Park" included office buildings, industrial buildings, retail facilities, and 4,400 apartment units, which combined would resemble a "city" with both a daytime and nighttime population. That resident population never materialized. A 2.7-mile-long dike was built high enough to turn back a 500-year flood. Millions of tons of earth were moved to protect Earth City.

233.0 Mighty, Muddy, Modified Missouri River

Just ahead you will cross the Mighty Missouri River. I-70 roughly parallels the Missouri River all the way across the state. Before the railroads were built, the Missouri River was the I-70 of its day. Trappers, explorers, and settlers traveled up this river. Cargo moved west to supply the settlers, and farm goods moved back to markets in the east. Lewis and Clark were among the throngs that used this riverine superhighway as they headed west, just as you are doing now. You are only about 30 miles from where it joins the Mississippi, nearly doubling the volume

Scene on the Missouri River.

Riverine highway (Missouri Department of Natural Resources)

of water in that river. From its headwaters in Montana, to the confluence with the Mississippi, the Missouri River travels 2,341 miles and drops 3,600 feet in elevation. Here you will see that the river has been modified for human use.

The Missouri is the world's largest reservoir system, with six reservoirs in four states providing irrigation, flood control, and consistent water levels for navigation. Thirty-five percent of the river's length has been impounded, and 32 percent has been channelized. Levees prevent flooding in bottomlands, 95 percent of which is now cropland. The U.S. Army Corps of Engineers maintains a 9-foot-deep, 735-mile-long shipping channel between Sioux City, Iowa, and St. Louis. These alterations shortened the river by 72 miles! The Missouri in its natural meandering state was America's longest river, but now that it has been shortened, it is almost exactly the same length as the Mississippi. The health of the river is threatened by sand and gravel mining, channelization, and pollution from the runoff of farms, factories, and cities. Japanese conservationist Tenaka Shozo said, "The care of rivers is not a matter of rivers, but of the human heart." Many hearts have turned to caring for the Missouri River. Groups like Missouri River Relief, the Missouri Watershed Information Network, the Coalition to Protect the Missouri River, and Friends of Big Muddy all work to keep the fish, wildlife, and people who depend on the river healthy and prosperous.

229.0 Nation's First Interstate

When President Eisenhower signed the Federal-Aid Highway Act in 1956, the Missouri State Highway Department was ready to spring into action and build its portion of the interstate system. The department had already made plans to improve portions of U.S. Highway 40 by upgrading it to a four-lane, controlled-access highway, so it was easy to relabel this project and include it in the new interstate program. On August 2, 1956, the Missouri State Highway Commission approved construction of this portion of Interstate 70. Within a few weeks of these contracts being let, a concrete roadway was poured along I-70 in St. Charles, making this stretch the first interstate highway.

228.0 St. Charles

In 1804, William Clark and his Corps of Discovery camped here for six days as they reloaded their supplies upon their keelboat and one of their pirogues, finished hiring the last of their crew members, and awaited the arrival of the other famous captain of the journey—Captain Meriwether Lewis. With the entire crew now assembled, they set off from here on their historic journey up the Missouri River to the Pacific. Thousands of travelers followed as St. Charles became the eastern end of stagecoach lines and a jumping-off point for supply shipments and travelers heading west to Kansas City and beyond.

As you drive west you will be paralleling the routes of many westward travelers who have gone before you. St. Charles was Missouri's first capital. While the permanent capitol was being built in centrally located Jefferson City, legislators needed a place to conduct governmental affairs. St. Charles was chosen after its citizens pledged free meeting space. On June 4, 1821, elected delegates met for the first time on the second floors of two adjoining buildings. These buildings provided space for the Senate and House, smaller quarters for the governor's office, and a meeting room. Heated debates about state's rights and slavery filled these rooms until 1826 when the building in Jefferson City was completed. To visit the first capitol, take Exit 228.

Weather radar

226.0 Weather Radar

The 12-foot-diameter white ball on the tower beyond the stores to the left, ahead at mile 225.0, once housed a weather radar. The Weather Forecast Office and radar moved here from Lambert International Airport in 1974. The radar was decommissioned in 1994. The site is now used by the City of St. Peters to broadcast their television station. Modern NEXRAD (Next Generation Radar) radars obtain precipitation and wind information based upon returned energy. The radar emits a burst of energy. If the energy strikes an object like a raindrop, the energy is scattered in all directions. A small fraction of that scattered energy is directed back toward the radar. Computers analyze the strength of the returned energy, the time it took to travel to the object and back, and the changes in it to determine the type and location of the object(s) struck. This process of emitting a signal, listening for any returned signal, then emitting the next signal takes place up to 1,300 times each second. Echoes from migrating birds regularly appear in spring and fall. Returns from swarms of insects and even bats are sometimes apparent during summer. Weather radars have saved an untold number of lives by tracking the movement of dangerous storms, thereby allowing people time to take shelter.

222.0 St. Peters

French trappers and traders settled here in the eighteenth century. German Catholics joined them in the early 1800s. The town of St. Peters was named after the first church in the area, a 35-by-25-foot log church built in 1815 called "St. Peters on Dardenne Creek." By the late 1800s the town had two railroad depots, hotels, saloons, and bustling shops. The church you see on the left is the Gothic-style All Saints Church, which was built in 1874 to replace the log church on Dardenne Creek because the creek frequently flooded, making it difficult for parishioners to get to church.

221.0 O'Fallon

This city was named for Maj. John O'Fallon, who was the nephew of explorer William Clark of Lewis and Clark fame. John O'Fallon became rich by buying and selling supplies to the army, then investing his newly acquired wealth in railroads. He was one of the promoters of the Pacific Railroad (later Missouri Pacific), the North Missouri Railroad (later the Wabash), and the Ohio and Mississippi Railroad (later Baltimore and Ohio), and he was also the first president of each of these railroads. Today most people would probably think of a railroad alongside their property as a noisy nuisance, but back in the mid-1800s people fought to have the trains come through their land. Railroads were essential for commerce and growth. Before highways, towns that were not on railroads or rivers seldom survived. A German immigrant, Judge Arnold Krekel of the U.S. District Court, welcomed the railroad through his property in 1854 and named the area for his friend O'Fallon in 1856.

During the Civil War, German immigrants formed a Union regiment to defend the North Missouri Railroad line because railroads were a popular target for the Confederacy. Arnold Krekel led the regiment, called Krekel's Dutch. Between 1990 and 2007 O'Fallon grew from 17,000 to 74,000 residents, and it is now the eighth-largest city in the state. O'Fallon is headquarters for MasterCard's Global Technology and Operations Center.

218.0 St. Charles County

You are driving through St. Charles County. Two famous frontiersmen settled in this county. Daniel and Rebecca Boone
settled about 20 miles south of here in 1799, and Jean Baptiste
Pointe du Sable, a fur trader of African descent who is often
considered to be the founder of Chicago, moved here a few
years after Boone. This county was organized by William Clark
as a district that extended north to Canada and west to the Pacific Ocean. Although the boundaries have shrunk, the county's
population continues to grow. St. Charles is the fastest-growing
county in Missouri.

214.0 Planned Town

To your left you can glimpse portions of Lake St. Louis. Lake
St. Louis is not only a lake, but it is also a town. In the 1960s its
founder R. T. Crow had visited two "new towns"—Reston, Virginia, and Columbia, Maryland. Unlike most towns that grow
from small settlements in an unplanned way, new towns are
complete communities designed and built around detailed master plans on previously undeveloped land. Crow believed this
area was an excellent location for a first-class new town. Lake
St. Louis became a city in 1975. As was anticipated by its developers, it is one of the fastest-growing towns in Missouri. Three-
time Grammy-winning rap and hip-hop singer and actor Nelly
has a home in Lake St. Louis.

213.0 Van Plant

The large brown building on the right horizon beyond the trees
is a GM assembly plant. Depending on the season, you may need
to look back over your shoulder at 211.8 to see the assembly center. This is a 3.7 million-square-foot facility (77 acres under one
roof). It is the only factory that produces the full-size Chevrolet
Express and GMC Savana vans. In recent years, this plant has
been the most productive large van plant in North America,
investing 24.4 hours of labor per vehicle, resulting in forty-two
vehicles produced per hour over two shifts.

212.0 Tires to Turn Turbines

The striped smokestack on the horizon to the right is the Ameren Sioux Power Plant. This coal-fired power plant was the first

in Missouri to burn chipped rubber tires to augment coal as a fuel source. This plant can burn more than 20,000 tons of tire chips annually—the equivalent of 25,000 tons of coal per year, thereby providing electricity for more than 4,000 residential customers. This consumes more than 2.5 million discarded tires each year. The tires from the vans made at the GM plant might end up here someday and help meet Missouri's energy needs. Ahead at mile 161 you will see an Ameren Power Plant that uses a nuclear reaction to heat the water, which makes the steam that turns turbines to create electricity.

209.0 Crossroads of the Nation

Wentzville calls itself "Crossroads of the Nation" because it is at the junction of I-70 and U.S. Highways 40 and 61, which becomes I-64. Between 2000 and 2004 the population of Wentzville grew by 41 percent, making it the second fastest-growing city in Missouri. The George Thorogood song, "Going Back to Wentzville," honors the fact that Wentzville is home to the legendary R&B and rock and roll icon Chuck Berry. Wentzville was founded in 1855 as a depot on the Northern Missouri Railroad. It was named after Erasmus Livingston Wentz, a railroad engineer for the line.

207.0 Weigh Station

The odd-looking poles that hang over the road ahead (206.2) signal a weigh station or a "chicken coop" as some truckers refer to them. These poles send a signal to a box the truckers have in their front window that lets truckers know whether they can pass through or must stop for an inspection. If their box turns green they can pass on through, but if it turns red they must stop. The first pole turns the box on, the second lets them know whether they have to stop, and the last pole next to the weigh station turns the box off. According to the Department of Revenue, "All commercial motor vehicles, except those licensed for 18,000 pounds or less or otherwise exempted by law, must stop at weigh stations unless so directed by an officer." These stations not only check the weight but also check if fuel taxes have been paid, if cargo is properly balanced, and if the driver is in proper condition for driving.

205.0 Foristell

Foristell is another railroad town. Settlement here began when the railroad was built in 1856. The community grew during the Civil War when a mill and a tobacco factory were established. The town is named after Pierre Foristell, a respected wealthy local farmer and cattle rancher.

204.0 Caterpillar

Ahead on the right you'll see a yellow and black CAT sign indicating one of more than 200 Caterpillar dealerships in the United States. Caterpillar is the world leader in construction and mining equipment, manufacturing over 300 different machines. Their largest dump truck will not be seen on I-70, because it is used only in mining. This truck is almost 24 feet high, 48 feet long (more than half a basketball court), and 30 feet wide—6 feet wider than the two lanes of I-70 that you are driving on. Caterpillar also makes engines for yachts and fishing boats, and it is the world's number one producer of electrical generators. The company was formed in 1925, but the two founders had been manufacturing steam and gas track-type tractors since the 1890s. The Allies used one of the first "Caterpillar tractors" in World War I. Caterpillar equipment helped build I-70 and highways around the world. Now Caterpillar is working on projects that are out of this world as they collaborate with NASA to build construction equipment to be used to build a permanent base on the moon.

202.0 Wright City

In 1857, Dr. Henry Wright platted this village along the newly constructed North Missouri Railroad. Then in 1863, Union soldiers raided Wright City and burned down the Baptist church, a blacksmith shop, and Kennedy's Saloon—all places where Southern sympathizers congregated. Wright City businesses benefited first by being along the railroad, then by being along U.S. Highway 40 (see mile 197.0), which ran through the center of town.

201.0 A Common County Name

You have entered Warren County. Warren is a common county name. At least thirteen eastern and midwestern states have a county named Warren, honoring General Joseph Warren, a Revolutionary War soldier who died at the Battle of Bunker Hill in Boston.

200.0 Good Greif

In the white building immediately to the left, the Greif Corporation manufactures paper drums. In 2007, more than 1.3 million drums were produced here! Some drums are sold to transport French's mustard and Worcestershire sauce from the factory to bottling plants. Others hold powders for pharmaceutical industries, spices for the meat industry, cheese, tomato paste, and other products. This plant is just one of 160 Greif locations in forty-five countries. Greif began as a cooperage shop in Cleveland in 1877, where wooden barrels, casks, and kegs were made. In those days all bulk foods and even fine wines were shipped in barrels. Early Greif kegs were so strong that they were used to deliver heavy spikes to railroads. Paper drums replaced wooden barrels because they were lighter. Today Greif also manufactures steel and plastic drums, corrugated containers, corrugated products for shipping protection, and dog food bags, as well as bottles for the water cooler industry.

199.0 Repeater Station

The brick bank building on the right was built in 1930 as a Bell System telephone repeater station. Repeater stations, now made obsolete by communication satellites, were the storehouses for equipment that strengthened the audio waves in long-distance phone calls, keeping conversations with friends and family audible and free of static interference. This repeater station was the first of three that were built between St. Louis and Kansas City. You will see another one ahead with its tower still intact at mile 53.

198.0 Interstate Ike

At this Rest Area and others ahead you can read the story of how, in 1956, President Eisenhower began the world's largest public works project—the U.S. Interstate System. The Interstate System was first designed as a military highway. President Eisenhower's experience in Europe during World War II impressed upon him the need for efficient highways to move soldiers and equipment. One of the goals of the Interstate Highway Act was to allow quick evacuations of cities with a population of 50,000 or more in the event of an attack. The Interstate System was born out of a fear of nuclear war, not with family vacation travel in mind. Eisenhower apparently imagined the ultimate rush hour, but probably never envisioned morning and evening rush hours that clog interstates in St. Louis and Kansas City.

197.0 America's Main Street

The road running along I-70 on the left is the old Route 40. Before Interstates, two-lane federal highways carried people cross-country. During the heyday of automobile travel in the 1950s, Route 40 stretched 3,220 miles between Atlantic City and San Francisco and carried more traffic than any other transcontinental highway. It is now about one-third shorter as it ends at the junction with Interstate 15 in Utah. Although the current U.S. 40 shares the pavement with I-70 in some places, it is still a significant highway in its own right for many stretches along its route. In 1811, long before the automobile, the eastern portion of what became U.S. 40 was part of the National Road, the first federally funded interstate road. Between 1926 and 1964, U.S. 40 brought millions of people from the East out into the Great Plains and mountain states. Because so many towns sprang up along U.S. 40, it has been called "America's Main Street." Old U.S. 40 nestles up against I-70 as a frontage road for much of the way across Missouri. You can still see abandoned gas stations (such as an abandoned single-pump station at mile 150 and the tall sign for King's Gas and Diesel on the north side of Exit 183, visible beginning at 184.4) and family-owned motels, some still surviving, that sprung up and thrived along America's Main Street.

195.0 Elbow Room

Warrenton ahead is the county seat of Warren County. Daniel Boone's daughter and son-in-law Flanders Callaway built a home south of here near the Missouri River. Daniel Boone spent time here and was said to have "found elbow room" in what is now Warren County. He was buried here in 1820. In the mid-1820s Daniel's son, Nathan, befriended a neighbor, Gottfried Duden,

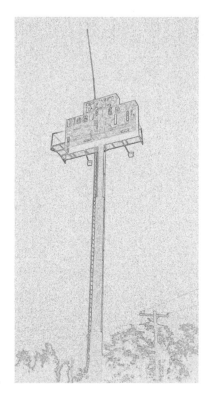

King Diesel sign

who influenced thousands of people to move to Missouri and fill up the countryside. Duden moved from Germany to Warren County in 1824 with the hopes of finding a place where his countrymen could escape from the social, economic, and political problems in Germany. In 1829, he published a report praising the democracy of the United States and the affordable land in Missouri. German emigrants, inspired by his report, settled here and throughout the state. Today residents are finding even less elbow room as the St. Louis metropolitan area encroaches into the county.

194.0 Boone's Lick Trail

This trail, which closely paralleled old U.S. 40 and I-70, ran due west from St. Charles across Warren County on what is now Highway M that goes through the south side of Wright City and into Warrenton's Main Street. It is considered to be the

Greeting the first train (Kansas City Public Library, Missouri)

grandfather of the Oregon and Santa Fe trails because travelers heading for those more famous trails used it. Originally called the Light Horse Trail, it was used by Indians, trappers, and fur traders. A lick is where salt occurs naturally in the ground. Elk, deer, bison, and other mammals came to lick the salt. Wolves, mountain lions, and humans that hunted these animals were attracted to these licks, too. It is called Boone's Lick because the trail led to a salt lick near Arrow Rock (mile 99) where Nathan Boone and his brother mined salt. The first stagecoach line traveled the trail in 1819, and it soon became the most traveled road in Missouri. Boone's Lick Trail was the I-70 of the 1800s as immigrants and livestock streamed west just as you are doing.

192.0 Railroads

Ahead on the left you'll soon see the Norfolk & Southern tracks. The importance of railroads cannot be overstated. Railroads moved people and products across Missouri, and they still do. The construction of railroads in Missouri started on a large scale in 1851 and affected every facet of life until the 1920s, when autos and paved highways finally crossed the country. Railroads determined land values and locations of towns. Missouri has 4,400 miles of main track, 2,500 miles of yard track, and about 7,000 crossings. A total of nineteen railroads operate in the state: four large national railroads; two regional railroads, which only operate in two or three states; two terminal railroads based in metropolitan areas; six short lines, regional railroads inside state lines; three tourist excursion trains; and Amtrak, which offers daily passenger trains between Kansas City and St. Louis. In April 1969 the body of President Eisenhower traveled along these tracks in a funeral car on its way to its final resting place in Abilene, Kansas.

190.0 Why Are Barns Red?

Ahead on the right, at 189.4, you will see a red barn. We often think of barns as being red. Why red? Some believe that farmers merely chose that color to provide sharp contrast with the green landscape. But a more accurate explanation may be that for many years the ingredients for red paint were cheap and easy to mix. Iron oxide powder would give a deep red color. Mixed in linseed oil, it could be spread on the barn boards. When a little casein (as in white glue) was added, the protective coating had a longer life. Casein adhesive comes from skimmed milk, which was always available on the farm. So, for generations, red barns were most common. With today's technology for formulating ready-to-use paint, white and other colors have become popular for painting barns. You will see more red barns ahead at mile 185.6.

188.0 Cropland

As you might guess by the white fence, Meadowlane Farm on the right used to be a horse farm. The unusual tall tower was used to observe and photograph the quarter horses working out on a track. Today this farm grows wheat, corn, and soybeans. Most of your trip across Missouri will be through farmland. The crop production mostly will be hay or grains. The hay crop comes from brome grass pastures. This nonnative grass is mowed two or three times during the growing season, baled, and then the bales (see mile 160) are moved to barns or feedlots. The grain crops include corn, sorghum, and wheat. Corn and sorghum are grass crops with long wide leaves on a single stalk. Corn grows 8 to 10 feet tall with ears on the stalk. Sorghum, also called "milo," is shorter and starts to produce a grain head at the top when it is about 10 inches tall. Winter wheat is planted in the fall and covers the entire field. It creates a bright green cover that becomes dormant in winter. In spring it grows again and brightens to a golden color for harvest time in early summer.

186.0 Montgomery County

You are now in Montgomery County. Like many Missouri counties, it is named after a Revolutionary War hero. Richard Montgomery was born in Ireland and served as a captain in the British army before settling in New York. He became a courageous officer in the Continental army and led troops that captured Montreal from the British, but later was killed attempting to conquer the city of Quebec.

185.0 Lifelines

In urban areas, concrete dividers separate the east- and westbound lanes of I-70. But here in the country, steel cables divide lanes whenever the median is between 36 and 60 feet wide and traffic exceeds 20,000 vehicles per day. Missouri is one of at least twenty-five states to invest in cables designed to block vehicles from crossing over the median into oncoming traffic. Although they cost $110,000 per mile to install and $12,000 per mile annually to maintain, these barriers have improved the safety of I-70. Crossover fatalities along Missouri's interstate highways dropped from fifty-five, the year before cables were installed, to two in 2007. Critics of these cables state that they can cause high-centered vehicles to flip upon impact, cause additional damage to cars involved in minor accidents, and prevent emergency vehicles from making U-turns to administer help. But overall, transportation safety professionals are convinced that these lifelines save lives.

184.0 Roadside Advertising

You have, without a doubt, read at least one billboard as you have traveled across I-70 today and maybe even used one to direct you to a business. You are one of about 42,000 people today who will view the billboards you see lined up on the left. These outdoor advertisements have been a point of controversy in Missouri. While billboards help travelers find services and help retailers and landowners gain revenue, others find them an eyesore on the landscape where they are believed to have become so abundant that it is difficult to see beyond the billboards.

According to the group Save Our Scenery, Missouri has 14,000 billboards—about three times as many per mile as eight neighboring states. It could be worse. The Missouri Department of Transportation Guidelines state that it is possible to have a billboard placed every 1,400 feet on the same side of the highway, which would allow a maximum of 950 billboards along the eastbound side of I-70 across Missouri and another 950 along the westbound side! In 2006, advertisers in the United States spent $6.8 billion on outdoor advertising and pay between $300 to $2,000 a month to promote their products along the roadways. Roadside advertising is nothing new. In 1872, the International Billboard Poster's Association of North America began right here in Missouri.

182.0 Laborer Learning

The Laborer's AGC Training Center, on the left, trains laborers; however, on more than one occasion careless sign readers have shown up with their Labradors seeking dog training. Courses are offered for construction laborers who are members of one of nine unions in eastern Missouri or are employed by contractors who contribute to a training fund. Participants live on-site for three to five days and choose from as many as sixty different courses, learn skills to work with cranes, power tools, aerial lifts, torches, pipes, and hazardous materials. Since the $5.4 million facility opened in 1986, 8,000 people have completed more than 26,000 courses.

181.0 Purveyors of Happiness

The huge bull, kiddie train, and 40-foot-high Ferris wheel on the right mark Tinsley's Amusements, which provides carnival rides for fairs and festivals. Read more about this Ferris wheel at 179E (page 133). On the right at the next exit the abandoned white and timber building with the red roof identifies this as an old Nickerson Farms store. Nickerson Farms created happy experiences for travelers along midwestern interstates from 1960 until the mid-1980s. Nickerson Farms was founded right here in Missouri by I. J. Nickerson, who worked for Stuckey's until he had a disagreement with W. S. Stuckey. He left Stuckey's and converted his Stuckey's franchise into the first Nickerson Farms. This roadside remnant, nostalgic to many travelers, was a place where families would fuel their cars (usually with Skelley's gas) and fill their stomachs at the restaurant. But the most distinctive and unique Nickerson Farm experience was watching bees make honey in the indoor beehive and then buying fresh honey in the gift shop.

180.0 Missouri Manufacturing

Ahead on the right is the Christy Minerals factory and on the left is the DuroFlex factory. Christy Minerals produces high-quality alumina silicate clays and calcines. Christy Minerals mines and processes clays for brick, tile, cement, floor tile, and ceramic industries. They not only make products to line walls of furnaces but also specialize in high-quality clay used by potters and other artisans. DuroFlex manufactures corrugated and fiberboard cartons, plastic shipping containers, plywood and fiberboard packaging components, and packaging for hazardous waste. Both of these companies ship their products all over the United States, so you may have a piece of pottery in your home made from Christy clay that came shipped in a box from DuroFlex.

178.0 Tree Farm

On the left is Hoette Farms & Nursery, a 420-acre wholesale nursery with over 180,000 ornamental, shade, and evergreen trees ready to be planted. The trees in this nursery, like other crops, are bred to resist disease or drought and to speed up growth rates. To harvest this crop, trees are machine-dug with large tree spades and placed in wire baskets with trunk protectors before being transported to the customer. Thomas Fuller said, "He that plants a tree loves others besides himself." The planting of a tree is a demonstration of hope and a gift of beauty to the next generation.

177.0 Hermann

Hermann (next exit) is a historic town on the banks of the Missouri River, 13 miles south of I-70. Wine making is not a new, trendy activity in Hermann. In 1837, German settlers founded Hermann, which eventually became home to sixty wineries. In 1848, Hermann held its first grape harvest festival and by 1856, Hermann was producing over 500,000 bottles of wine per year! Vines from Missouri were sent to both European and California vineyards, in the 1870s and 1890s respectively, to help rebuild

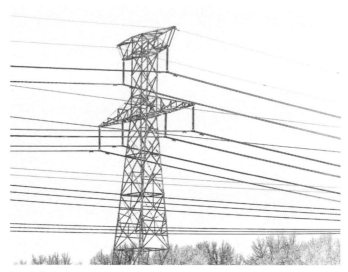

Power lines

their pest-infected vineyards. In the 1880s, Missouri was second only to New York in U.S. wine production. Today Hermann is home to four wineries. Artifacts from nineteenth-century German Americana are displayed at the Deutschheim Historic Site. Visitors can see home interiors, tools, and garden plantings, including grapevines planted 150 years ago!

174.0 Power Lines

The power lines crossing the highway ahead bring power from the Callaway Nuclear Power Plant (mile 162) to a substation at Montgomery City north of I-70. From there the power enters a grid that serves 1.2 million customers all over central and eastern Missouri from the Bootheel to the Iowa border. Power lines are constructed to carry different amounts of electricity. One measure of power is voltage, or pressure that moves current through the lines. To move electricity through your home takes 115 volts. About 6,900 volts are used to move power through lines along city streets or out to farms. To send power across Missouri requires much bigger lines. The electric line here carries 345,000 volts. You can tell the line carries high voltage because the cables are spaced far apart and long insulators attach the cables to the tower frames. Those insulators are a string of

George Baughman, hermit of Graham Cave (Montgomery County Historical Society)

ceramic bells hooked together to assure that the high voltage will not cause the current to jump across. In your home wiring, this is accomplished with a layer of insulating tape. As voltage increases, it requires a greater and greater separation. So when you see an electric line, notice how long the insulators suspending the cables are; the longer they are, the higher the voltage. Along with longer insulators it takes bigger cables to carry more power. The heavier cables demand larger and stronger towers to support the lines. Electricity travels great distances before reaching our homes.

172.0 The Cave State

Missouri is called the "Cave State" because it is home to 6,200 caves. At Exit 170 you can visit one of these caves at Graham Cave State Park, a National Historic Landmark on the banks of the Loutre River. Evidence points toward humans occupying this cave 10,000 years ago. A more recent cave dweller here was George Baughman who arrived in the 1880s. "George the Hermit," as he became known, was on his way to Pikes Peak to search for gold with a wagon pulled by two oxen. While camped near Danville, one ox died and the other ran off. While searching for the wayward oxen, George discovered a cave. He took up living in the cave and told people he was commissioned by the emperor of France to dig up gold hidden in the surrounding hills. He dug more than thirty shafts with only a pick and shovel, one pit being 75 feet deep. He stopped at that depth only because he did not want to take the gold out until the French emperor sent troops to protect him and the gold. He prepared a long petition to the emperor to send troops for his protection. When George's health failed, the proud hermit agreed to accept help from the county only upon being assured that the subsistence was merely a loan and that as soon as he took the gold out he could repay the loan. In fact, when people brought him food he would insist on giving them something—anything—even a squirrel skin in return. Alas, the French troops never came and the gold was never found. George the Hermit is buried near his cave.

Look for an old white building (once the chapel of the Danville Female Academy) next to the highway in the trees on the right at 170.8. You can read about this historic Civil War–era building at 170E (page 131).

169.0 Forest Benefits

The forested Loutre River valley provides many beneficial services. Besides the products mentioned at 82E (pages 104–105) and 152E (page 126), forests protect hillsides from erosion, thereby keeping streams and rivers clean. These forests filter the air to make it cleaner and healthier, and they remove greenhouse gases associated with global warming. They provide habitat for many of Missouri's 730 types of wildlife, including species that were nearly extinct such as deer, turkey, and wood ducks. When the leaves change color in the fall, the cool emerald forests explode in an inferno of reds and yellows. Because of the forest's beauty, Missouri's outdoor recreation and tourism industry is centered in forested regions of the state. This is another of the many ways these forests contribute to the state's economy.

168.0 Loutre River

You just crossed the Loutre River. *Loutre* in French means "otter." Early French trappers must have encountered the river otter in this river they named "Loutre." Today you can encounter

Danville Female Academy

otters in every county in Missouri, but this wasn't always the case. In 1980, it was estimated that there were somewhere between thirty-five to seventy otters left in the state. The Missouri Department of Conservation (MDC) planned to bring back the otter by trading Missouri turkeys for Louisiana otters. In the eleven-year program the MDC released 845 otters in forty-three streams across thirty-five counties. The reintroduction was a great success, but maybe too much of a success. The otter population in Missouri rose to 15,000 only twenty years after the first few creatures put their webbed feet on Missouri soil. These voracious eaters, capable of eating two to three pounds of fish each day, found their way into farm ponds and began devouring the landlocked fish. To keep a balance and manage these successful creatures, the MDC started a trapping season in 1996 that brought the population down to a little over 10,000 otters. Today in most streams you can find about one otter per mile.

165.0 The Kingdom of Callaway

Callaway County is named for Captain James Callaway, grandson of Daniel Boone, who fought in the War of 1812. Callaway and three of his men were killed in an Indian ambush while crossing the Loutre River in 1815 in what is now neighboring

Montgomery County. The bodies of the three soldiers were cut into many pieces and so were buried in a common grave, whereas Callaway's body was found several days later by a search party that included his father, who had come from St. Charles County to help look for it. Since the Civil War, this county has been referred to as the Kingdom of Callaway. Several accounts exist regarding how the county came to be known as a kingdom, but all accounts point to the fanatical Southern sympathies of the residents, some promoting the secession of Missouri from the Union. In 1861, Union troops advanced toward Fulton where all the young men were away at war. To protect their town from Yankee pillaging, the old men and boys used bravery and cunning. Armed with only their hunting rifles, they painted some logs black to look like cannons and lined them up for the Union to see. Union General John B. Henderson negotiated with Colonel Jefferson Franklin Jones and agreed not to invade Callaway if the colonel disbanded his men and their "artillery." This amounted to the county negotiating a treaty as a sovereign state with the U.S. government. Locals interpreted this treaty as recognizing their county's independence and right to govern itself as its own kingdom. The city ahead, called Kingdom City, reflects that you have entered the Kingdom of Callaway.

162.0 Power to the People

Over the next 12 miles on the left horizon you can see the 553-foot-tall hourglass-shaped cooling tower of the Callaway Nuclear Power Plant. On cold winter days a plume of steam will make it easier to locate. As noted back at mile 212, power plants, whether coal-fired or nuclear, heat water to make steam to turn turbines that create electricity. Water from the Missouri River is pumped 5 miles to the plant through a 48-inch-diameter underground pipe. After being heated to create the steam, the water goes to the cooling tower. The tower can cool 585,000 gallons per minute from 125 degrees to 95 degrees. About 15,000 gallons per minute are lost out the top through evaporation and another 5,000 gallons per minute are sent back to the Missouri River. The Callaway Nuclear Power Plant creates enough electricity each year to meet the energy needs of more than 840,000 households.

160.0 Windmills

Off to the far right by the silver grain bins is a windmill. No, it is not a fan to keep the cattle cool (as some city slickers have reportedly thought). Windmills are another way of capturing energy and putting it to work. Farmers harness the wind to lift groundwater from a well to the surface for use as drinking water for cattle, and occasionally for garden irrigation and household uses. Windmills allowed settlers to live, grow crops, and raise livestock away from the edge of lakes, rivers, or streams.

159.0 Don't Treat Soil Like Dirt

Agronomists study soil and take it seriously. To them, what you see covering these croplands on the right is not dirt; it's soil. They say dirt is what's under your bed or fingernails. Dirt is misplaced soil. Soil is a mixture of very small particles worn from rocks, dead and decaying plants and animals (called organic matter), water, air, and billions of living organisms—most of which are microscopic creatures called "decomposers." Decomposers are part of nature's cycle of life and death that function by converting dead organic matter into chemicals that can be taken up and used by living things. By making organic nutrients available, they improve the soil's fertility. Good soil is *alive* and keeps other things, including humans, alive. People concerned about soil conservation take the long-term view of the popular conservation slogan that "we do not inherit the land from our fathers; we are borrowing it from our children."

158.0 Big Bales

The big round bales you may see rolled up in the fields or stacked near a farmstead are hay bales. This hay will be used to feed cattle in the winter. They can weigh a ton! Often they weigh at least 2,000 pounds. Until the invention of the baler in 1968, hay was gathered loose and pitched to the cattle with a fork. Crews went from farm to farm to compact hay into 60-pound bales, thus making it easier to stack and transport. But handling those bales required a lot of backbreaking labor and the compacting plunger injured many farmers. Today, there is an entire industry associated with making and selling balers and associated equipment that has eliminated tedious, difficult hand labor, making it possible for fewer workers to supply our food at lower cost.

156.0 "Where Caring Counts"

This is the motto of Missouri Girls Town, seen on the left, a residential treatment facility for girls, ages eight to twenty-one, who have been abused or neglected. The mission is to create a loving, stable environment for the girls and help them develop the life skills they will need as adults. The General Federation of Missouri Women's Clubs founded Missouri Girls Town in 1953. Each year Girls Town provides care for nearly 100 girls from across Missouri. Before coming to Girls Town, the typical girl has already been through nine failed placements that may have included foster care, hospitalization, and failed adoptions. That a town named "Bachelor" (because of its high population of single men when it was founded) is near a place called "Girls Town" is mere serendipity.

155.0 Farm Pond Fun

Ponds such as the one you see ahead on the left at 154.0 provide drinking water for livestock and store water runoff, thereby reducing soil erosion. But ponds offer many recreation benefits as well. They offer excellent fishing opportunities, not just for children, but for serious anglers. Seven of Missouri's record fish came from farm ponds, including the biggest white crappie, black crappie, and bluegill. Missouri leads the nation with more than 300,000 private ponds and lakes. The Missouri Department of Conservation (MDC) will stock private ponds at no cost as long as they meet certain criteria, such as being at least eight feet deep. The MDC stocks about 650 ponds (1,000 acres of water) annually. Typical stocking rates are 100 bass, 500 bluegill, and 100 catfish for every surface acre of water. Within two or three years, these ponds produce keeper-sized fish and lots of fun.

154.0 River of Mud

Luckily for you, a nicely paved bridge passes over the Auxvasse Creek as you travel I-70. Before such concrete conveniences, a group of Frenchmen traveled through this area with Lilburn Boggs, who later became a Missouri governor. Upon crossing the river, they became stuck in the mud and so aptly named the waterway the *Riviere aux Vases,* which translates to "River of Mud."

153.0 Callaway Livestock Center

Ahead on the left just beyond the overpass is the Callaway Livestock Center where John Payne Harrison and his son sell more than 124,000 head of cattle each year. John grew up in the cattle sales business. It is the only life he has ever known and he never thought about doing anything else. The first livestock sale in Callaway County was held on February 1, 1876, and a weekly livestock sale has been held here ever since. In 1876, the sales commission earned by the auctioneer was 2.5 percent. It has never changed and is still 2.5 percent today. The Callaway Livestock Center has been in the Harrison family since 1904. In the early days mules were sold and then driven to Mississippi by teenage boys, some as young as fourteen years old. The mules would follow the boy and a white horse with a cowbell around its neck. John still has the cowbell that led the mules to Mississippi. Today most livestock comes from within a 100-mile radius, but some cattle come from as far away as Illinois and Nebraska to be sold. Cattle bought here are shipped all over the United States.

151.0 The Missouri Farm

The Missouri Farm on your left is not your typical family farm. Instead it is a private research farm where scientists conduct studies to improve agricultural production. You may have noticed the silver structures on many farms. These are grain storage bins. Here at the Missouri Farm you see what are nicknamed "spiderweb" bins because of the central tower with multiple chutes radiating out and down from it. After harvest, grain is elevated from trucks by a conveyor in the central tower. The grain is then directed into the appropriate chute and down into the round bin.

150.0 Winston Churchill Memorial

If you take Exit 148 south for nine miles to Fulton, you can visit the Winston Churchill Memorial, placed where Churchill made his famous "Iron Curtain" speech in 1946. With help from President Harry Truman, the president of Westminster College, Franc L. McCluer, scheduled Churchill to speak at the school. Churchill had recently ended his first tenure as British prime minister and agreed to speak in Fulton. Before his speech he dined on country ham and fried chicken at the home of McCluer, and eloquently declared, "The pig has reached its highest point of evolution in this ham." On March 5, 1946, a crowd estimated at 25,000 people came out to hear his speech, "The Sinews of Peace." National media descended upon the town, and the speech was broadcast live on each of the four national radio networks. As Churchill spoke of the threat of Soviet Communism in post–World War II Europe, he told the crowd, "From Stettin in the Baltic to Trieste in the Adriatic, an iron curtain has descended across the continent." Although, at the time, most people doubted such a growth of Soviet Communism, Churchill had accurately predicted, from the little town of Fulton, Missouri, changes that would affect the whole world.

149.0 Firefighters Memorial

At the Mid Missouri Tourism Center (Exit 148) you can see a memorial and a museum dedicated to Missouri firefighters (see photo on page 125). To your right you can see a larger-than-life sculpture of a firefighter with head in hand and on bended knee. You can step along the bricks that pave the "Walk of Honor" and lead you to the memorial wall that lists the names of firefighters who have died in the line of duty. Fred Turnbull, of the St. Louis Volunteer Fire Department, begins the list that extends from 1838 through the present decade. A 2-by-3-foot piece of the World Trade Center is also on display.

147.0 Super Soakers

Ahead on the right are irrigation systems stretching out above the crops. They are called center pivot rigs. The long arm, mounted on wheels, slowly sweeps around the field pivoting from the center where water enters. Pumps deliver water from a well to feed the arm. Water flows out through the long arm with hanging sprinkler heads aimed at plant roots to reduce evaporation loss. Electric motors drive the wheels very slowly so the arm makes one revolution in twenty-four hours or longer, sprinkling the crop within the circle. Many arms are a quarter-mile long and cover 130 acres. But some irrigation arms extend for a half mile, thereby watering 568 acres out of the 640 acres in a square-mile field.

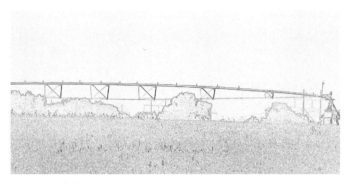

Center pivot irrigation rig

145.0 Tucker Prairie

On the left is the Tucker Prairie Natural Area. This 146-acre prairie is owned by the University of Missouri and is used for class projects and research on such topics as the effects of haying and burning on grassland plants. The word "prairie" comes from the French word for a grassy meadow. When Europeans first traveled to Missouri, prairie grasses and wildflowers blanketed 15 million acres (one-third of the state). Today only 90,000 acres of this original prairie remain. But these remnants are amazingly diverse. Over 800 plant species occur in Missouri prairies, and 224 different kinds of plants have been found on Tucker Prairie. At the next rest stop (mile 105) you can see prairie grasses and wildflowers up close in a small restored prairie.

144.0 Advertising Barns

The old barn on the right ahead at mile 143 is being used as an advertisement for Meramec Caverns. In the early 1930s, the owner of Meramec Caverns took a trip to Florida looking for construction work. Along the way he noticed all the signs painted on barns encouraging travelers to "See Rock City" or "Chew Mail Pouch Tobacco" (on more than 50,000 barns). He decided to use barn painting for the Caverns. During the heyday of barn advertisements in the 1950s, more than 300 barns in twenty-six states from Michigan to California had signs for Meramec Caverns. Originally in return for allowing the Meramec Caverns sign to be painted on their barn, the barn owner was given a railroad pocket watch, the wife was given a box of chocolates, and the whole family was given a free pass into Meramec Cave. But the biggest incentive was that the entire barn would receive a fresh coat of paint. As barns disappear such ads are becoming scarce. Zoning and roadside beautification laws prevent new ads from being painted. Only eighty-two Meramec barns in five states remain. Hobbyists travel all over the United States searching for and photographing the few remaining advertising barns. As a side note, the early owner of Meramec Caverns is credited with inventing the bumper sticker. Cardboard "bumper signs" were tied onto visitors' bumpers with twine. Soon they began experimenting with different adhesives. Early versions had wax paper backing that would be peeled off to expose flypaper-like glue. In the 1960s politicians made bumper stickers commonplace but also created bad feelings by using glue that made them difficult to remove.

142.0 Soybeans

Some fields along this stretch of I-70 are soybean fields. During summer look for rows of short rounded plants. The plants appear bushy until the beans are ripe and the rounded leaves fall off, leaving a two-foot-high brown stalk with pods aligned in rows. Like corn products, you use soybean products every day. Hundreds of food products use protein-rich soymilk or flour. Other products such as candles, crayons, ink, body lotions, shampoos, hair conditioners, paint removers, and fabric conditioners are made from soybeans. Soybeans now are used to make biodiesel, a renewable fuel that is clean burning. Missouri is "home to soy biodiesel" as the original testing was done at the University of Missouri. Other states provide energy from their oil fields, but Missouri provides fuel from its soybean fields. We are not the first society to use the soybean. The Chinese discovered this plant 2,000 years ago and by 220 A.D. they were making soymilk and tofu.

141.0 Growing Farm Fun

On the right is the big red and green barn of the Shryocks' Callaway Farm. This family farm has been in operation since 1889. Today two brothers, their sons, and their families run it. They grow corn and soybeans on the 850-acre farm, but their fields also produce a healthy crop of fun. They offer hayrides, camp-fires, and amazing mazes cut into cornfields. Many farmers are supplementing their traditional farm income by opening their farms to the public for agriculture-based recreation. This new industry is called "agritourism."

140.0 Little Dixie

The Little Dixie Wildlife Area is 4 miles south of Exit 137. This region along the Missouri River is known as "Little Dixie" because the residents were immigrants from Kentucky, Tennessee, Virginia, and the Carolinas. In 1860, 114,931 slaves lived in Missouri. This area had the highest percentage of slaves. Slaves mostly worked on farms. Most farms were along the Missouri River because of the rich floodplain soils and ease of shipping products down the river. Therefore most slaves were in the river counties through which you have been driving. Lafayette County had the most with 6,374 because of thriving hemp farms. Boone County had 5,034, Saline 4,876, and Callaway 4,523 slaves. Unlike the Deep South where plantations held many slaves, these farms were small so Missouri farmers usually had only one or two slaves. At the beginning of the Civil War many slaves fled their owners and set up their own self-reliant villages in this area.

139.0 Roadside Wildflowers

Ralph Waldo Emerson said, "The earth laughs in flowers." Over the next few miles, notice how during summer the rights of way laugh in wildflowers. In early summer you will likely see the light blue flowers of chicory. Chicory roots were used to make a coffee substitute during World War II and are still used in some trendy coffees. The white flowers are Queen Anne's lace, named because the cluster of small flowers gives a lace-like appearance, complete with a dark red flower where the queen pricked her finger while sewing. It is also called wild carrot because it is a member of the carrot family and the root smells like a carrot. Yellow flowers here are mostly black-eyed Susans. A tea made from black-eyed Susans was used as a folk medicine, and a yellow dye can be made from it. In the fall you may see purple-colored asters and the brilliant yellow goldenrod—a plant falsely accused of causing hay fever.

137.0 Boone County

This county was named for the famous trailblazer and wilderness scout Daniel Boone, who claimed, "I have never been lost, but I will admit to being confused for several weeks." Although Boone is famous for his wilderness adventures in Kentucky, he moved to Missouri when he was sixty-five years old, and some say that he spent the best years of his life here where he could explore new lands not yet crowded with people. In his twenty-one years in Missouri, he saw the land change dramatically. When he first arrived in 1799 this land was ruled by Spain. Within a year of his arrival, France took ownership. Four years after his arrival, the United States finally claimed it in the Louisiana Purchase. Always looking for adventure, Boone was more often exploring the wilderness than settling in one place. When he died in 1820, his family buried him next to his wife in what is now Warren County. But in the 1840s a cemetery company from Frankfort, Kentucky, took the remains of Boone and his wife back to Kentucky. The Boone family donated the gravestone to Central Methodist University in Fayette with the stipulation that the stone would never leave the campus. It is fitting that even after death Daniel traveled through his beloved forests on his way back to Kentucky.

134.0 Yellow Signs

Along the highway fence lines, you may have noticed tent-shaped yellow signs with black numbers on them such as these on the right. Utility companies use these signs to mark underground natural gas or oil pipelines or other corridors. The signs are angled so that the numbers are markers for airplanes searching for leaks, vegetation that needs to be removed, unauthorized construction, or other encroachments in the corridor. The orange signs along the fence mark the fiber-optic communication cables. These colors, along with blue for water, are the commonly used colors to indicate the type of buried utility.

132.0 Capital Highway

The next exit (128) takes you south to Jefferson City, the capital of Missouri. Although I-70 misses this state capital by 30 miles, it passes through four other state capitals—the capitals of Colorado, Kansas, Indiana, and Ohio. Can you name them?

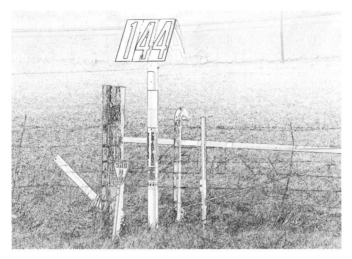

Utility sign

131.0 Hominy Creek

In 1896 this creek gained its culinary name from the settlers here
who raised corn and made it into lye hominy. Hominy consists
of dried corn kernels that have been soaked in lye so that hulls
are removed. Once the hard outer hull is removed the germ is
easier to digest, more nutritious, and often considered tastier.
As far back as 1500 to 1200 B.C., hominy was eaten in what is
now Guatemala. Many Native Americans and the early colonists
ate hominy. Hominy is boiled until cooked and served as either
a cereal or vegetable. Hominy may also be pressed into patties
and fried. Hominy ground into small grains is called "hominy
grits." Hominy grits are a favorite food in the southern United
States. In fact Georgia named it the "Official State Prepared
Food." The Charleston *Post and Courier* said that "a man full of
grits is a man of peace."

FROM COLUMBIA TO KANSAS CITY

130.0 Mizzou

Exit 128 takes you to the University of Missouri campus (MU),
which was founded in 1839, making it the first public university

west of the Mississippi River and the first state university in Thomas Jefferson's Louisiana Purchase territory. MU's tiger mascot was inspired by and named after a local Civil War militia called the Missouri Tigers. Today it is known as "Truman Tiger" in honor of Missouri's only U.S. president, Harry Truman. A distinctive feature of the campus is a row of six Ionic columns. These columns were part of the first building on campus, built between 1840 and 1843. This building burned to the ground in 1892 in a fire rumored to have been caused by the first electric lightbulb west of the Mississippi River. More than 5,000 trees and 650 varieties of plants accent the 1,358-acre campus with colorful flowers and, in the fall, brilliant leaves. The campus features eighteen buildings on the National Register of Historic Places, 600-year-old Chinese stone lions, and Thomas Jefferson's original tombstone. The student body is made up of more than 28,000 students from all fifty states and more than 100 countries. MU is widely known for its programs in journalism (the world's first journalism school was founded here in 1908), and such well-known current broadcast journalists as Jim Lehrer and Elizabeth Vargas graduated from here. Brad Pitt majored in journalism here with a focus on advertising. He left college two credits short of graduating to move to California. Other famous alumni include singer Sheryl Crow, actors George C. Scott and Tom Berenger, businessmen Edward D. Jones (founder of the investment firm) and Sam Walton (founder of Wal-Mart), and cartoonist Mort Walker, who created *Beetle Bailey*. A life-size statue of Beetle stands in front of the campus Alumni Center.

127.0 Hail Columbia

Several magazines and websites including *Money Magazine*, *Men's Journal*, and MSN.com have ranked Columbia as one of the best places to live. The name "Columbia" refers to Christopher Columbus and was the first popular name for our country. Many early leaders wanted the United States of America to be named "Columbia" because it was shorter and more poetic. Columbia became the female personification of America, similar to the male Uncle Sam. Today she is most often seen at the beginning of a movie made by Columbia Pictures. Nicknames for this city include "The Athens of Missouri" and "College Town USA" because it is home to three universities. Besides the University of Missouri, Stephens College and Columbia College are located in Columbia. Stephens College is a women's liberal arts college with particularly strong programs in fashion design, dance, and theater. Many Stephens students have gone on to excel on stage and screen, including such notables as Joan Crawford, Elizabeth Mitchell, Jennifer Tilly, Dawn Wells, and Paula Zahn. Columbia College also started out as a women's school, but it is now coed. Columbia College specializes in adult and military education. It serves nearly 25,000 college students each year at thirty-two campuses in eleven states, with fifteen campuses being located on military bases. As with most college towns, Columbia is known for its eclectic mix of restaurants, shops, art galleries, music venues, and coffeehouses.

124.0 Silent No More

Ahead you will see a sign indicating that the next 54 miles is dedicated to those who have served in the "Silent Service"—submarine veterans. Why 54 miles? This length represents one mile for each of the fifty-two submarines lost in World War II and one mile each for the USS *Thresher* and USS *Scorpion* lost during the Cold War. Submarine veterans hope to have the entire length of I-70 from Maryland to Utah designated as Submarine Veterans Memorial Highway.

123.0 Perche Creek

Two hundred years ago this creek was named "Split Rock" or *roche perche* in French. The most common story of how the creek got its name was from a "pierced rock" that was observed by William Clark on June 6, 1804. High on a limestone cliff, a cave-like hole can still be seen today from the Katy Trail (see mile 101). Because of radical shifts of the Missouri River over time, this interesting rock, once at the original mouth of the creek, is now separated from the Missouri River by a mile.

122.0 Pork Place

On the right, just before the exit, is the headquarters of the Missouri Pork Association, where they support promotion, research, education, and legislation all aimed at getting people to "fork more pork." Missouri is seventh among states in pork production, producing 6 percent of the nation's "other white meat." This industry employs 25,000 Missourians and contributes more than $1 billion to the Missouri economy. Sometimes pigs *do* fly—15 out of every 100 hogs are exported!

121.0 Redcedars

The evergreen trees you see along the highway on the hillsides to the right are eastern redcedar. Redcedars are not really cedars but instead a member of the juniper family. They grow in open and sunny places and often encroach into grasslands unless they are burned. Although ranchers do not like them because they compete with the grass, redcedars have many positive attributes. Because of its color, fragrance, and presumed ability to repel moths, redcedar wood is used for chests, wardrobes, and closet linings. Cedarwood oil is used for making many other fragrances. Woodenware and many of the wooden novelties sold at tourist attractions are made from redcedar. At one time most wooden pencils were made from redcedar and the tree was known as pencil cedar, but now only about 10 percent of pencils are made from this tree. Redcedars are in the top five trees used for Christmas trees. Redcedars benefit wildlife as they provide year-round shelter from predators and the elements. Birds use them for nest sites and redcedar berries are eaten by many kinds of birds as well as raccoons, skunks, foxes, rabbits, and other mammals. A redcedar found on an undisturbed rocky bluff in Missouri has been estimated to be well over 1,000 years old!

119.0 Corps of Discovery

Along the highway you'll see brown signs indicating the Lewis and Clark Trail. Their "trail" was the Missouri River, and they traveled it across the state from the confluence of the Mississippi and Missouri through Kansas City in 1804. Thomas Jefferson sent Meriwether Lewis, William Clark, and their "Corps of Discovery" to explore the newly acquired Louisiana Purchase and search for a water route to the Pacific Ocean. Along the way they discovered animals, plants, and peoples. Their journals reveal details of these discoveries. For example, on June 6, 1804, very near the spot where you will cross the Missouri just ahead, William Clark wrote that they saw "some buffalow Sign to day." This was their first mention of the 2,000-pound, 6-foot-tall creature that once roamed Missouri. You won't find such signs today. By the 1840s all of Missouri's buffalo (more accurately called American Bison) had been killed for their hides and meat. Travel always involves discovery to those who take the time to notice things. Our hope is that you will be part of a "corps of discovery" as you drive across Missouri.

117.0 Wine Country

Some vineyards can be seen briefly on the left. Exit 115 leads to Rocheport, a river town filled with historic nineteenth-century buildings. On the way you will pass the Les Bourgeois Winery and the associated vineyards. Wine tasting and tours are available, along with a bistro with a bluff-top view of I-70 and the Missouri River. This is just one of Missouri's forty-seven wineries. The vineyards represent some of the 1,100 acres of grapes grown in Missouri. In 2003, more than 3.6 million bottles of Missouri wines were sold, bringing in $26 million in sales, $2 million in state tax revenue, and creating more than 250 jobs. A recent legislative proclamation named Norton/Cynthiana the official grape of Missouri.

116.0 "Too Thick to Drink, Too Thin to Plow"

That is how settlers described the muddy Missouri River. You will cross the Big Muddy ahead at mile 115. As you cross the cantilevered through truss bridge, if traffic allows, glance back over your shoulder to see the spectacular white cliffs rising above the river. These cliffs were mentioned by Lewis and Clark in their journals and contain pictographs left by Native Americans. For centuries the river served as both a highway and hunting, trapping, and fishing resource for Native Americans and settlers. Today this river is still a national treasure that serves mankind in many ways, including providing us with hydroelectric power, vital irrigation water, and transport for barges carrying asphalt, cement, sand, and grains such as wheat, soybeans, and corn. Jet skis, johnboats, and aluminum canoes ply the waters that had been navigated by dugout canoes of Native Americans and the steamships of settlers. The Mighty Mo' has also been a source of inspiration for poets and artists. When Walt Whitman experienced the river in 1865 he wrote,

Others may praise what they like;
But I, from the banks of the running Missouri, praise nothing
    in art,
Till it has well inhaled the atmosphere of this river, also the
    western prairie-scent,
And exudes it all again.

Even now as you cross the river you might be able to get a sense of the atmosphere of the powerful and inspiring Missouri River.

114.0 Floodplains, Flood Protection

Just after you cross the Missouri River you will cross the river's expansive floodplain, which includes the Big Muddy National Wildlife Refuge, established in 1994. We often think of floods as being bad, but here on the refuge floods are a great event. Floods create wetland habitats for wildlife and contribute rich nutrients to bottomland soils. Floodplains serve as enormous water storage areas in times of flooding. The low, flat area you pass over can become a lake during times of high water. Cutting the river off with levees from these natural storage areas increases flooding downstream. Allowing the river to leave its banks and expand into these plains reduces downstream flooding. Evidence of floodplain benefits is mounting in Missouri. The flood of 1993 forced more than 10,000 people from their homes and resulted in dozens of deaths and billions in property damage. After that flood government agencies purchased more than 21,000 acres of floodplains in Missouri. Some levees were moved back away from the river and other areas were left open to future flooding. In 1995 and 2002, torrential rainstorms caused the National Weather Service to predict floods along the Missouri. But these floods never happened as the river had more room to spread out. Things generally turn out better when instead of trying to corral Mother Nature, we let her "go with the flow."

Clydesdale farm

112.0 Kings of the Road

Look to the right, just before Exit 111 (111.8) to catch a glimpse of a stately long white fence surrounding a 350-acre farm. This farm is the world's largest breeding facility for the famous Anheuser-Busch Clydesdales. In 2008, the horses moved from Menifee, California, to be closer to the brewery's St. Louis headquarters, but for privacy of the horses, this facility is not open to the public. Up to 150 horses, mostly breed mares and geldings, reside here. Before they pulled the signature red and gold beer wagon, this six-foot-tall, 2,000-pound breed bore powerful farm horses along the River Clyde which was in a valley, or "dale," in Lanarkshire, Scotland. The large lovable horses have been a part of Budweiser's "King of Beers" history since 1933, when August Busch Jr. presented his father with a gift of six Clydesdales and a wagon to carry the first case of post-Prohibition beer from their brewery. Today, the Clydesdales bring smiles to millions of people as their impressive 20-inch horseshoe-clad hooves pound the pavement in celebrations across the country from NASCAR and Super Bowl events to Main Street parades.

110.0 Cooper County

You are in Cooper County, named after Benjamin Cooper. Cooper was born in Virginia, but moved to Kentucky and then Missouri as the frontier boundaries moved west. He was a colonel in the militia and was an associate of Daniel Boone during the Indian Wars. He first moved to this area with his wife and five sons in 1808. However, Governor Meriwether Lewis (of Lewis and Clark fame) ordered him to abandon his farm and return east because he was too far into Indian country and away from protection in the event of an Indian attack. He complied with Governor Lewis and relocated near the Loutre River (mile 168), but two years later he returned here with settlers from Kentucky, Tennessee, and Virginia.

109.0 Prairie Home

As you travel west you are leaving the eastern forests behind and entering a landscape that once was prairie. The next exit (106.6) invites you to travel south to a little town called "Prairie Home." The comforting name invokes images of a gentle, quiet town surrounded by wide-open rolling grasslands braided with colorful wildflowers—a place where complete strangers would greet your arrival with a glass of cool lemonade and friendly conversation. This friendly name is what the founders of the Prairie Home Institute hoped would draw students to their college prep school when they named it "Prairie Home" in 1864. The town was established ten years later and named after the school. The institute was strategically built along the main highway between Boonville and Jefferson City, and its founders proudly advertised it as a learning environment "separated from the expense and vice of city schools." The college is now gone, but the town is still peacefully nestled among the rolling hills. At the next rest stop you can see a piece of prairie in a planting of prairie wildflowers and grasses.

107.0 Santa Fe Trail

A brown marker at mile 101.4 indicates that this stretch of I-70 is part of the Santa Fe Heritage Trail. An ancient Indian trail, known as the Osage Trace, followed along the Missouri River from the Mississippi. As settlers used and improved it, the Trace became the eastern part of the Santa Fe Trail and eventually U.S. Highway 24 in Missouri. In 1821, William Becknell, the "Father of the Santa Fe Trail," organized and led the first trip over what would be America's first and foremost commercial highway for the next sixty years. This journey left from Franklin, a town now lost to the shifting Missouri River. (Note that Exit 106 takes you to the town of "New Franklin.") Becknell returned having made a 5,000 percent profit from the trip. The 900-mile trade route created a new market for the goods from Missouri.

Most of the trade was in cotton cloth as up until that time the residents of Santa Fe wore clothes made from coarse material or animal skins. Trail travel also started the Missouri mule industry. By 1826, mules brought from California replaced horses on the trail because horses lacked the necessary endurance. But by 1829 traders upgraded their beasts of burden again as oxen replaced mules because oxen were stronger than the mules. The outfitting and "push-off" site continued to move west along with settlements and improved roads. By 1831, Independence, 100 miles upriver, was the starting point for trail travelers. Later it became Westport in what is now Kansas City. Soldiers and military supplies traveled it during and after the Mexican-American War. During just one travel season (April 24 through October 1, 1860), the following commercial trail traffic was recorded at a toll bridge in Kansas: 3,519 men, 2,667 wagons, 478 horses, 5,819 mules, 22,738 oxen, 61 carriages, and 6,819 tons of freight. These numbers only include those involved in the freight business. They do not include emigrants or other private business travelers. In 1880, the expansion of the railroad to New Mexico ended traffic on the trail.

102.0 Boon or Boone?

The historic river town of Boonville is named after the famous pioneer Daniel Boone. But notice on the large blue water tower to the right that there is no "e" in this town's name. Daniel's relatives were inconsistent in the spelling of their own name. Early maps of the area spelled it with and without the "e," too, probably following the inconsistent Boone family. Daniel's tombstone read "Boon" without the "e" and with the "N" carved backward. As noted back at mile 137 the gravestone resides at Central Methodist University's Stephens Museum in Fayette. You can take Exit 102 up to Fayetteville to see it for yourself.

101.0 From Rail to Trail

Just ahead a modern day trail crosses above I-70 on an old railroad bridge. The Katy Trail carried freight trains instead of wagon trains, but today hikers and bikers travel the trail. The Katy Trail was built on the abandoned corridor of the Missouri-Kansas-Texas Railroad (the MKT or Katy line). You may have already noticed signs for this 225-mile-long hiking and biking trail as it has intersected I-70 twice between here and St. Louis. This trail is managed as a state park and people can hop aboard the Katy at twenty-six different trailheads or two fully restored depots. Many progressive states and towns have converted their abandoned railroad rights-of-way to recreational trails, but the Katy Trail is the world's longest rail trail.

100.0 Cooper County Fairgrounds

Ahead at mile 99.8 on the right (just past the overpass), you will see the Cooper County Fairgrounds. This fairground is unique in that the land is privately owned by a volunteer group and was purchased with funds donated from the community to "encourage youth to show their talents and grow in the agricultural community." When someone was awarded money for their "best of show," they often generously contributed their winnings back to the Fair Board. By the early 1960s, those funds enabled the Cooper County Agricultural and Mechanical Society to buy this land. Competitions reward youth who have worked hard grooming their animals and growing their crops. Besides competitions, county fairs entertain families with auctions, tractor pulls, greased-pig-chasing contests, carnival rides, and deep-fried fair food (the last two of which should never be mixed). A county fair brings rural communities together. It is a time for community members to socialize, foster community pride, and share and compare the fruits of their labors—products raised on their land or prepared in their kitchens. To read more about county fairs see 98E (page 110).

99.0 Arrow Rock

Exit 98 takes you to historic and quaint Arrow Rock. Today only seventy-nine people live in Arrow Rock, but it was once a bustling town. Founded in 1829, Arrow Rock is where the steamship met the wagon—the intersection of the Santa Fe Trail and Missouri River—making it the largest river shipping town between St. Louis and Kansas City. By 1837, four warehouses along Arrow Rock's landing were supplying the southern United States with agricultural products and Missouri mules. The railroad took the steam out of steamboat travel, and the river channel gradually receded east. Arrow Rock saw its last ferry run in

Bustling Arrow Rock, circa 1910 (Missouri Department of Natural Resources)

1927. Arrow Rock is a National Historic Landmark and has been called the "most historic spot in Missouri." It is home to Missouri's first state historic site, quaint shops, restaurants, and the historic Lyceum Theatre, Missouri's oldest regional professional theater. The name "Arrow Rock" came about because an outcropping of flint along the river made it an important manufacturing area for arrow points by Native Americans.

98.0   Fertile Fields

The collection of farm equipment on the right at Exit 98 belongs to the Fertilizer Dealer Supply store. This firm sells sprayers, fertilizer spreaders, and liquid fertilizer applicators. Such machinery is necessary because nutrients in the soil are taken up by plant roots and converted into the standing crops. Whenever crops are harvested, the nutrients, now in the form of plant material, leave the fields by the truckloads. Many farmers must use chemical fertilizers to replace nutrients lost each year. You may see chemical tanks (often white) being pulled by tractors or parked by farmsteads. Applying too much fertilizer has caused pollution of groundwater used for drinking in some areas. Fortunately, farmers are developing better techniques that maintain soil fertility for future generations of farmers while producing a bountiful crop today. Besides adding chemicals, one strategy is to leave the dead plant residue from the previous season on the field to hold the soil and to reestablish the natural cycle of decaying plant matter going back into the soil. This "no-till" agriculture not only helps hold the rich topsoil in place but also puts nutrients back in the soil naturally. Look for crop stubble left in the fields during fall and winter.

96.0   Chouteau Creek

It seems fitting that this creek with the famous name is near the middle of the state. The Chouteau family had a huge role in settling Missouri from St. Louis to Kansas City. In 1764, young Auguste Chouteau helped his stepfather, Pierre Laclede, set up a trading post and build the city of St. Louis. In 1821, Auguste's nephew, François Chouteau, established a trading post at the confluence of the Kansas and Missouri rivers that began the growth of present-day Kansas City. Amazing that we so quickly cross over a tiny creek that honors such a grand family—the family that helped establish the two largest cities in Missouri.

95.0   Rocks Going to the Sea

Because rainwater moves soil particles into streams and rivers that ultimately flow to the sea, and because soil is made of tiny particles worn from rocks, people say soil is "rocks on their way to the sea." This washing away of soil particles is called erosion. Unfortunately, Missouri ranks third in the nation in soil loss due to erosion. One hundred million tons of soil erode in Missouri annually. This volume of soil would cover all four lanes of I-70 from Kansas City to St. Louis 35 feet deep! The movement of soil into the sea by wind and water is inevitable, but farmers delay the trip and save their precious topsoil by applying soil conservation techniques to slow the water runoff and hold soil particles in place. Farmers reduce erosion through strategies such as contour plowing (making furrows across the slope), planting grass strips in drainages, leaving crop residue on the surface, creating raised ridges called "terraces" (notice on left after 94.0 and at many other places ahead) that catch rainwater and allow it to soak into the soil, or leaving a buffer zone of vegetation along streams. By preventing soil from moving toward the sea, farmers keep their cropland productive and Missouri's streams clean. You can see these techniques being used many times in the miles ahead.

93.0 Get the Lead Out

The Lamine River is a 70-mile-long tributary of the Missouri River. According to Samuel Cole, an early area resident, the last hunting and trapping expedition Boone took before he died in September 1820 was to the mouth of the Lamine River. The name "Lamine" is believed to have come from French explorer Sieur de Bourgmond, who wrote in 1714 that "Indians take lead from a mine." By 1720 maps identified it as "Riviere a la Mine" or "River of the Mine." By 1850, Missouri had lead mines throughout the southeast, southwest, and central parts of the state. Today, 92 percent of the United States' primary lead supply comes from Missouri, and it is one of the top producers in the world.

92.0 Where Ozarks Meet Prairie

For the next few miles enjoy your last glimpses of the rocky Ozark terrain to your left. These Ozark hills are the remnants of America's oldest mountain range. Rock cuts along the highway will give way to wide-open Osage Plains. Ice formed the Plains and fire formed the Ozarks. The fertile land north of the Missouri River was scoured by glaciers and left with windblown loess (pronounced "luss") soil, whereas the Ozarks's core was formed by volcanic mountains, before wind and water shaped the valleys and cliffs that give this land its signature beauty. The hilly Ozarks feature forests and pastures for grazing cattle, whereas in the Osage Plains you will see mostly cropland. It is too difficult to cultivate crops in the thin rocky Ozark soil, but in the Osage Plains crops thrive on the deep soils.

91.0 On the Curve

After going nearly straight for about 160 miles, this terrain forces I-70 to take a wide, sweeping S-curve to avoid six river crossings in the next 8 miles. Bridge construction and maintenance are expensive, so a one-mile curve to avoid the meandering Lamine River was more efficient than building all of those bridges. Missouri, the state "Where the Rivers Run," has fifty-five major river bridges, the most of any state. It is all uphill from here. The elevation in this river valley is 524 feet above sea level. You will climb to 760 feet above sea level at Kansas City.

89.0 Smooth Sumac

On the right side of the highway between 88.4 and 88.2 you will notice smooth sumac covering the hillside like miniature trees. You'll recognize it by its long, skinny leaflets that droop almost like palm leaves. Hillsides are perfect places for this shrub whose extensive root system prevents erosion. By mid-July, sumac has produced its dark red velvety fruits that are a treat for at least thirty-two species of birds. When mixed with sugar and water, the crushed fruit also produces a surprisingly refreshing drink. Native Americans used the fruits to treat fever, the leaves to smoke, and the entire plant for staining and dyeing. While most people don't notice sumac much in the summer, they can't help but see it in the fall. When the green leaves turn to a deep scarlet red the sumac is the first "tree" to signal that fall has arrived.

88.0 Cell Tower Cluster

This "grove" of cell phone towers is one of several clusters at high points along I-70. Only twenty years ago cell phones and towers did not exist, but today you probably have a phone with you as you read this. During the 1990s about 5,000 towers were erected per year, and between 2000 and 2002, towers registered with the FCC (only a small fraction of all towers) increased from 69,000 to 138,000. New towers continue to pop up like weeds all over the landscape. See 87E to learn how cell phone towers kill birds and how new tower designs can limit bird collisions.

87.0 Salt Water in Missouri

You are entering Saline County, named for the salty springs in the area. The town of Sweet Springs ahead is named for nearby springs that are not salty. Settlers sometimes referred to good-tasting, nonsalty water as being "sweet." When Lewis and Clark passed by Salt Creek they noted, "So many licks and salt springs on its banks that the water of the creek is brackish. . . . One bushel of the water is said to make 7 pounds of good salt." As noted at 194W, Daniel Boone's sons shipped salt from this region, giving it the name "Boone's Lick Country." They boiled

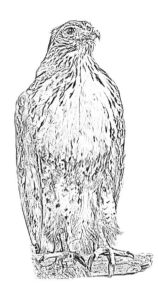

Red-tailed hawk

the salty water until it was sludge. Then it was dried and sent downriver to St. Louis. Salt was a critical resource used for preserving food and tanning leather.

85.0 Highway Hawks

As you drive along you will see large hawks sitting on fences or trees along the highway. Most will be red-tailed hawks. They are common year-round wherever there are trees. Red-tails are attracted to the highway because the grassy median and rights-of-way provide ideal habitat for their favorite food—mice and other small mammals. Although some people call them "chicken hawks," they do not bother chickens. In fact, red-tailed hawks are valuable to farmers because they eat rodents that in turn would eat the farmer's grain. Look for a mostly white breast and short, fan-shaped tail that may be brown or rusty-red depending on the age of the bird. The large black birds seen soaring with wings upturned into a V-shape are turkey vultures. To learn more about these roadside scavengers see 108E (page 112).

83.0 "Wood" You Believe What Comes from Wood?

As you pass through this wooded area you'll see different kinds of trees such as oak, cottonwood, and walnut. Besides the many wood products mentioned at 82E (page 104), more than 5,000 other products are made from the fibers and chemicals in wood. "Woody" products that may be traveling with you today include the gum you're chewing and the paper it's wrapped in; the crayons and coloring book the kids are using in the backseat; your suitcase; the toothpaste, cosmetics, prescription drugs, soap, shoes, and shoe polish in your suitcase; sandwich bags and the dried fruit inside them; your ice cream snack, tea, or coffee; disposable diapers, the car upholstery, the rubber in your tires, your vehicle's paint, and the steering wheel that guides you!

80.0 A Plethora of Poultry

The long buildings ahead on the right at 79.4 are part of Chris and Heidi Rogers's poultry farm. At any one time 150,000 broilers are being raised here. Chicks arrive by the truckload when they are only three hours old. They must be hand-fed for the first four days. When they are eight weeks old they get shipped to the Tyson plant in Sedalia, Missouri. There is no such thing as a holiday for the hardworking Rogers family as the chickens require daily care. Their greatest challenge is keeping the chicks alive in the excessive heat in the summer and cold temperatures in the winter.

78.0 Road Rock

The quarry ahead on the right is one of more than 900 quarries worldwide owned by the LaFarge Corporation. Twice each month explosives blast the limestone layers into small pieces. Between 2,000 to 3,000 tons of rock per day and more than 500,000 tons of rock each year are removed from the quarry. Most of it is applied to county roads within 40 miles of the quarry.

77.0 Rock Cut

You can see the limestone layers up close in the roadside rock cuts. Limestone is composed of sediments that settled to the bottom of an ancient sea that covered this part of North America. The layers here are mostly remains of sea animals such as mollusks and corals that died and fell to the bottom. As you speed past this wall of ancient creatures you are passing stories in the stones and fascinating finds. Uniform circles on a rock could be the roots of a prehistoric plant. Ancient coral leaves a pattern that looks like honeycomb. A white spot with wavy edges could reveal shark teeth, and a small cylindrical piece with a hole in the middle could be a stem of a crinoid. As mentioned in the Introduction, this is Missouri's state fossil. Rock cuts are time machines that reveal the past.

75.0 Corncob Pipes

Over the next two miles you will cruise pass several cornfields. Corn is America's number one crop. In 2006, Missouri growers harvested over 2.6 million acres of corn, producing 363 million bushels, with a value of more than $1.1 billion to this state's economy. Many amazing items are produced from corn (see 72E [page 102] for a list of surprising corn products and facts), but one item produced exclusively in Missouri rests on mantels and reading tables around the world. It is the Missouri Meerschaum, otherwise known as the corncob pipe. The Missouri Meerschaum Company is the world's oldest and largest manufacturer of the corncob pipe. In 1869 Henry Tibbe applied plaster to the pipe bowl to better absorb tar and juices. This plaster was similar to Meerschaum, a type of clay used in high-grade pipes, and so Tibbe declared his pipe to be the Missouri Meerschaum. Mark Twain commended the refined bowl when he told a fellow writer, "This, sir, is not a corn cob pipe. It is a 'Missouri Meerschaum.'" Besides Twain, many famous characters, both fictional and historic, smoked corncob pipes, including Tom Sawyer, Popeye, Frosty the Snowman, Davy Crockett, General Pershing, General Douglas MacArthur, and entertainers Arthur Godfrey and Tennessee Ernie Ford. In fact, MacArthur designed a special corncob pipe that was made to his exact specifications.

Pipe corn is grown along the Missouri River in eastern Missouri. The University of Missouri created a smaller corncob for pipe production. One cob produces up to five pipe bowls. Antique machinery must be used for harvest because modern combines destroy the cobs. Cobs are dried for two years, then sawed and finished.

Author Christopher Morley compared the corncob pipe and its local owners when he said,

Missouri's reputation for incredulity may be due to the corncob habit. One who is accustomed to consider an argument

*General Douglas
MacArthur
and his corncob pipe
(Missouri
Meerschaum Co.)*

over a burning nest of tobacco, with the smoke fuming upward
in a placid haze, will not accept any dogma too immediately.
. . . A Missouri meerschaum whose bowl is browned and
whose fiber stem is frayed and stringy with biting betrays a
meditative and reasonable owner. He will have pondered all
aspects of life and be equally ready to denounce any of them,
but without bitterness.

He also wrote this poem:

THE PIPE OF PEACE
What is the magic Of a corncob pipe?
No matter how peevish or irritable
My husband may be,—When he is smoking his
    Missouri Meerschaum
He will do anything I ask.
Couldn't something about corncob pipes Be put in The
marriage ceremony?

71.0 Fireplace

The brick chimney with the TV antenna still attached, at 70.6, is
all that remains from a three-bedroom home that was destroyed

Brick chimney

by an electrical fire in February 2001. The homeowner drives past this spot twice each day on her way to and from work. She leaves the chimney standing as a reminder of the fire that changed her life saying,

This was the first, and only, home I have ever purchased. To lose the house was devastating, but more devastating was to lose the contents inside the home that can never be replaced—the pictures, yearbooks, childhood toys and family furniture. Those are the things I think about each time I drive past on I-70. To lose everything is hard to overcome and I still feel sad. Some day when I purchase another home I will take down the chimney and use the bricks to build a fire pit in the back yard. And if I never buy another home the chimney will remain standing as a reminder.

She has rebuilt her life and moved on with a new appreciation for the things she has and a deeper sympathy for victims of disasters whose homes are destroyed.

69.0   Terrific Terraces

On the right, the farm fields have been terraced. For the next 30 miles you will see many terraced fields. As mentioned back at mile 95, farmers make terraces in their fields to slow the run-off from rainfall or melting snow. They plow mounds or ridges of soil to curve along a slope, making level areas to hold the moisture so it will soak into the soil for better crop production. When water runoff is slowed, less soil is carried away, preserving topsoil and reducing erosion. Farmers make parallel terraces of equal width so that an equal number of crop rows can be planted, thus making it easier to operate tractors, combines, and tillage tools. Long gentle curves aid in making terraces farmable using commercial farm equipment. Just building the terrace does not assure erosion control. Farmers must regularly maintain the terrace shape and restore ridge height.

67.0   Disappearing Barns

Off to the right is an abandoned, dilapidated barn. You will see several old barns along I-70. Strong construction of barns makes it more difficult to tear them down. Since space is abundant here in the county, farmers let time and the elements take them down. Barns are becoming less common. Large modern tractors and combines no longer fit through the doors, old dirt floors are not hygienic enough for modern milking operations, and enormous round bales of hay no longer need a loft. Although many farm families have a sentimental attachment to their old wooden barns, such barns do not earn any money for the farmer so they fall into neglect, particularly in this day of big corporations taking over small family farms. And few craftsmen exist that would know how to fix a barn, even if the owner wanted to save it. Some encourage their conversion into artist studios or bed-and-breakfasts. Others believe these are just other ways of destroying an old barn. Organizations are popping up all over the country to save barns. *Successful Farming* magazine and the National Trust for Historic Preservation have a program called "Barn Again!" This program helps farmers rehabilitate their historic barns and put them back into productive use. Enjoy these beautiful and functional buildings while you can.

65.0 **"La Fayette, We Are Here."**

In 2 miles you will be entering Lafayette County, named after Marie-Joseph Paul Yves Roch Gilbert du Motier. Yes, that is the name of just one person, a man also known as the Marquis de La Fayette. It is a good thing he had this title because his full name would not fit on the historical markers and other city signs honoring this defender of liberty. La Fayette joined the French army at fourteen years old. As a nineteen-year-old officer, against the warnings of his friends and even Benjamin Franklin, then the U.S. envoy to France, La Fayette risked his life to come to America to fight in the Revolutionary War. The British sent two ships to capture him, but he escaped using a disguise. After a two-month journey he landed safely in South Carolina. Upon arrival, this teenage officer received an honorary rank of major general in the American army. He refused his salary and led his men to battle as a volunteer. He became a lifelong friend of George Washington and named a son after him. After the war, La Fayette returned to France and played a prominent and colorful role in French history during the French Revolution. During World War II, when General Patton visited La Fayette's grave in France, he said, "La Fayette, we are here"—a reference to the U.S. army repaying the debt owed to La Fayette for his service to America. In 2002, President George W. Bush made La Fayette an honorary U.S. citizen.

63.0 **Emma**

The town with the quaint name of "Emma" was named for the daughter of the original postmaster, a Reverend Demetrio, who was also the pastor of Holy Cross Lutheran Church. No other town in 1880 in Missouri was named "Emma," and so the postmaster general approved it. The U.S. Postal Service controlled the names of new post offices and hence influenced the official names of most new towns.

62.0 **St. John Cemetery**

On the right side of the road, amid the corn, you will see a white iron archway (61.2) that frames the road that leads back to a white picket fence surrounding St. John Cemetery—the final resting place of Civil War veterans and eight men who were killed by "bushwhackers." Bushwhackers were ragtag ren-egade groups of men with Southern sympathies who roamed the countryside looting and burning farms and villages. The names on the tombstones, both old and new, reflect the German heritage of the area. Beneath the moss on several of the aging stones are German inscriptions and unique engravings of weeping willows, hands pointing to heaven, and the crown of life. The local United Church of Christ was founded on this land in 1850, and the first burial was in 1853. The church was later moved to Emma.

61.0 Silos

Silos, such as the ones you'll see on both sides of I-70 over the next few miles, are part of the rural skyline. These tall cylindri-cal structures store feed for cattle at both beef and dairy farms. They vary in height from 30 to 100 feet and from 20 to 40 feet in diameter. Silos are filled in late summer and fall with feed for cattle to eat during the winter. In fall, corn or a grain sor-ghum that has partially dried stalks may be chopped into fod-der (a coarse feed). When placed in a silo, this fodder ensiles or cures into traditional silage. Silos may also be filled with high-moisture corn that has been harvested by combines early in the fall. Chopped grass crops are cut from fields and when packed in airtight silos the grass cures somewhat like sauerkraut to be-come haylage, delectable cattle feed. You can see two kinds of silos along I-70: gray cement silos (here on the right) and dark blue steel silos. Gray concrete silos like the one here often have a silver-colored aluminum dome top. Concrete silos are un-loaded from a mechanism at the top that throws the feed down a chute along the side of the silo to wagons or conveyors. The domed top covers the unloader. With this type of unloader, the first feed taken out was the last that was put in. The deep-blue steel silos ahead on both sides of the road are called by their trade name "Harvestore." Like other silos they store grain for cattle feed, but these glass-lined steel silos are filled from the top. Unlike cement silos, Harvestores have nearly flat roofs be-cause they are unloaded from the bottom, so they do not need to cover an unloader at the top. Harvestores use bottom unload-ers so that the first grain loaded in is the first taken out.

59.0 Concordia

German immigrants settled Concordia in 1860. Concordia means "harmony," but its early days were anything but harmonious. On October 10, 1864, bushwhackers killed twenty-five men from this town. Most German settlers opposed slavery and so were targeted by the bushwhackers. As William Quantrill's group of guerrillas neared Concordia, a group of townspeople rode out to meet them (near mile 62 in present-day Emma). Twenty-one men from Concordia lost their lives and four more were killed in their homes. Some of these men were laid to rest in St. Paul Lutheran Cemetery, ahead on your left. Fifteen Civil War soldiers are also buried there. Ahead on a hill to your left you'll see the campus of St. Paul Lutheran High School, the second-oldest Lutheran high school in America. Read more about this school, which was established as a Lutheran college in 1883, in 57E.

56.0 Beautiful Barns

At 55.4 notice the lovely white barn on the right, partially hidden by the trees. As you have traveled across Missouri you have seen dozens of barns representing many sizes and shapes and you will see many more between here and Kansas City. Family farms needed a building where they could house and care for livestock and store grain and equipment. Many barns had a Gambrel roof recognized by its two ridges added parallel to the center gable ridge making a steep slope down below the flatter upper slope. This design created a high open loft to store hay. Under haylofts, wagons could be pulled inside and unloaded. Shed attachments on the sides might include workhorse stalls, a small animal pen for baby animals, a shed dedicated to stanchions for eight to twelve milk cows, and a feed room. The turrets at the top of the barns are ventilators designed with flues to supply fresh air to the dairy cows. A farmstead may have included a chicken house, storage shed, silo, and silver grain storage bins. As mentioned back at mile 67, barns are slowly becoming obsolete. But for many decades barns like this white one were the focus for the farm "factory," which took the raw materials from the fields and turned them into dairy products, meat, and other foods for our tables.

54.0 Aullville

At Exit 52 Aullville is named after the Aull brothers. The brothers formed the J. & R. Aull Company, and between 1822 and 1836 John, James, and Robert Aull outfitted pioneers with goods as they traveled west. If they were still in business you could stop at their general store for some coffee, a sunbonnet, stick candy, a cloth doll, or tools in case your wagon (or station wagon) had a breakdown. General stores were sometimes the only businesses in a town and the storekeeper could double as banker and mailman. Many people would barter for their goods or promise to repay debts as they traveled west, but unfortunately time lapses between shipments of goods from the east and debtors not repaying their loans caused the Aull Company to go bankrupt in 1836.

53.0 Microwave Tower

The huge tower on the left is what remains of an obsolete ATT microwave communications tower. It was part of a nationwide network of such towers that handled long-distance phone calls. The brick building was built to withstand severe storms or sabotage. It contained equipment that allowed you to call people all over the country as your call was sent from tower to tower. Communication satellites and fiber-optic cables have made the tower obsolete. In fact, three fiber-optic communication cables run from St. Louis to Kansas City within the I-70 right-of-way: one along the north edge, one along the south edge, and one right down the middle. Cars are not the only things speeding along this stretch of highway—information and messages are too. This is a real information highway!

52.0 Highway to History

Route 13 (Exit 49) ahead takes you to several historic sites associated with the Civil War. Most noteworthy is the Battle of Lexington State Historic Site (19 miles north). A Union Army of 2,700 men occupied the pro-Southern town of Lexington. As the Southern army advanced to take back the prosperous river town, their numbers swelled from the initial 7,200 to 10,000 to 12,000 as throngs of proslavery locals joined the ranks. With the strains of "Dixie" in the air, the Southerners surrounded and attacked the Union troops. The house of Oliver Anderson,

Battle of the Hemp Bales (Battle of Lexington State Historic Site, Missouri)

a slave owner and hemp farmer, was serving as a Union hospital. In spite of it being a hospital, it changed hands three times during the bloody three-day battle. The house survived and can be visited today. The battle has been called the Battle of the Hemp Bales. The Southerners had discovered hemp bales in a warehouse and arranged these bales in a line. They then began rolling the bales toward the Union line of trenches using them as giant shields. The Union cannonballs had little effect on the dense bales. By early afternoon, the line of bales had rolled up close enough to the Union trenches for a charge. After a brief but bloody hand-to-hand fight the Union army surrendered. The casualty count was 25 Confederate soldiers killed and 75 wounded, and 39 Union soldiers killed and 120 wounded. On the way up to the battlefield you will pass the Confederate Memorial State Historic Site. Opened in 1891, the Confederate Soldiers Home was home to more than 1,600 veterans of the Confederate army and their families and widows who found a place of rest here in their old age. These veterans were from all over the South and had fought in every major battle of the Civil War. The last of these former rebel soldiers, John T. Graves, died here in 1950 at the age of 108. The Civil War may have ended in 1865, but the "Lost Cause" lived on for decades in memories and stories of the old soldiers here at the Confederate Soldiers Home. President

Harry Truman visited the site twice to honor the 40,000 Missouri soldiers who served in the Confederate army.

48.0 Man's Best Friend

Sixteen miles south is the town of Warrensburg. It was here that the popular phrase "Man's Best Friend" originated about a dearly loved hound dog named Old Drum. A full-size bronze statue of Old Drum stands on the lawn of the Johnson County Courthouse. Read about Old Drum and the origin of the phrase "Man's Best Friend" at 49E (page 94).

47.0 Slowing Water

Immediately on the right you can see the grass waterways (strips of grass lining low areas in cropland) that slow water runoff and prevent it from carrying away soil toward the sea as mentioned back at mile 95. For the next 20 miles you will see more grass waterways as well as ponds that collect moving water. Erosion from an area covered in grass is 4,000 times less than erosion from bare ground. Look for strips of grass lining the low drainages in the cultivated fields ahead at 46.0 and 45.6 on the right.

46.0 Buried Treasure

The grass waterways and terraces that you will see ahead protect our soil. Our soil is a national treasure. President Franklin D. Roosevelt correctly said, "The nation that destroys its soil, destroys itself." Throughout history civilizations have prospered because of their fertile soil. When they abused their soil these civilizations crumbled. Our welfare is linked to the soil because nutrient-rich soil grows healthy plants, which in turn supports healthy wildlife populations, healthy livestock, and healthy human populations. Good soil grows bountiful crops, healthy animals, and prosperous people. Without good rich soil our nation would be "dirt poor."

45.0 Tall Tank

The blue water tower on the right belongs to Public Water Supply District No. 2. It stores 100,000 gallons of water, 135 feet above the ground. The water stored here is pumped from Higginsville City Lake about 10 miles away. When the lake is low, supplemental water is pumped from the Missouri River, 15 miles

Grass waterway

north of Higginsville. The water from this tank goes under I-70 to serve 300 to 400 people living south of the interstate. The district rents the top of the tank to ATT/Sprint as a cell phone tower. If you are talking on the phone as you drive down I-70, your voice may be transmitted from the top of this water tank.

42.0 Fast Track

The I-70 Race Track at Exit 41 is known as the "Fastest Weekly Short Track in the World." This track hosts races in six classes with cars reaching speeds of 140 mph—twice your speed limit on I-70. The curves on this half-mile oval have steep 30-degree banks making it difficult to stand or walk on them, but easier to drive on them at high speed. Famous NASCAR drivers such as Rusty Wallace, Jeff Gordon, Kenny Schrader, Tony Stewart, and the late Adam Petty have raced here. In fact, this is where the late Adam Petty won his first race. Rather than speeding down I-70, you can take a spin on the raceway either with a driver or driving yourself. It will be much safer.

40.0 Family Farm

From 1959 to 2000 the pretty Ridgewood Farm on the right was a dairy farm featuring award-winning red and white Holsteins instead of the more common black and white variety. Dairy cattle from this farm were exported to Europe, Japan, and South America. In 1967, this farm produced a Grand Champion at the

World Dairy Expo. The milking operation was shut down when it became too expensive and time-consuming to maintain. Today Ron (who grew up on the farm) and Lisa Williams have 1,400 acres of corn, soybeans, and wheat and 120 head of beef cattle.

39.0 Odessa

Ahead is the town of Odessa. In 1880 the townspeople of Kirkpatrick were searching for a new town name because founder John Kirkpatrick did not want to risk attaching his name to a town he thought would fail. T. B. Blackstone, president of the Chicago & Alton Railroad, noticed the area's gentle hills and told the people how these rolling wheat fields reminded him of the city Odessa in the Ukraine. His inspiration gave the town a new name. If today Kirkpatrick could see this thriving community of over 9,000 people, perhaps he would regret removing his name from a town that did not fail after all. If you are traveling during the first full weekend of August you can stop for the annual Puddle Jumper Days festival. This fun event celebrates a train called a "puddle jumper," which made stops between Odessa and nearby towns in the early 1900s. A puddle jumper (also called a "doodlebug") was a self-propelled passenger-carrying railcar. Most were built in the 1910s and 1920s. The last ones quit running around 1960.

38.0 Lake Venita

On the left side of the highway as you go down the hill at 37.2 you can glimpse Lake Venita, a humble little remnant of a popular resort between Kansas City and St. Louis in the "roaring 1920s." Originally dedicated as Mulvill Lake on April 3, 1908, town founder and landowner John Kirkpatrick renamed it "Venita" for his niece. Cottages, boats, a beach, and a dancing pavilion provided highway travelers a place to relax along the water by day and dance by night. Today, Dyer Park still provides pleasure for the people of Odessa. Locals and travelers enjoy fishing, baseball, a children's playground, and an annual rodeo. Even though the cabins have been gone for over thirty years, travelers can spend the evening in tents while dancing music still echoes through the night—although square dancing (Missouri's state dance) has replaced the Charleston.

36.0 Ritchie Brothers Auction

Ritchie Brothers Truck Auction ahead on the left is just one of 110 locations in more than twenty-five countries. Ritchie Brothers is the world's largest auctioneer of industrial equipment, employing almost 1,000 full-time employees. The company holds public auctions to sell used and unused industrial equipment from the construction, transportation, marine, mining, forestry, petroleum, real estate, and agricultural industries. It was established in 1958 in British Columbia, Canada. You may see bulldozers, cement mixers, or cranes for sale here. In 2007, they held 350 auctions with gross proceeds of more than $3 billion.

34.0 Wrong Way Creek

As you cross over the Sni-a-bar (SNEYE-uh-bahr) Creek be grateful for modern conveniences of travel—for well-marked highways and detailed road maps. Sni-a-bar Creek was once a tricky waterway that fooled at least one trapper so that he steered off the Missouri River and traveled quite a distance before he realized his mistake. This is one of several stories of how the creek got its name. In an account of Stephen Harriman Long's expedition to the Rocky Mountains in 1823, we learn the story about the lost trapper "au Barre" and the tricky "Cheny au Barre" (note the phonetic similarity) that misled him. "Sni" seems to have come from variations of "channel," which is "chenal" in French, and "a-bar" seems to come from the trapper's name. You should have no such worries about taking a wrong turn on the well-marked I-70.

33.0 Farm-to-Market Roads

On the sign ahead you'll see the exit for highways Z and D. You may have already crinkled your brow at these lettered highways and then wondered if you hadn't already passed these two highways a few counties ago. In fact you did pass a Highway Z at mile 134 and a DD at mile 137. Even lifelong residents of Missouri have lost bets as to whether these alphabet highways were state or county roads. Because these names are repeated in different counties for entirely different roads, you'd think these narrow two-lane highways must be county roads. But these "farm-to-market" highways are owned and maintained by the

Missouri Department of Transportation. In 1952, a gasoline tax allowed the state to connect the rural communities with other towns and to put a state-maintained road within two miles of more than 95 percent of all "rural family units." Twelve thousand miles of county roads suddenly gained state status and an alphabet name. The problem is that twenty-two alphabet letters just can't cover the entire state. The letters G, I, Q, S, and X are not used because they can be confused with similar letters. So, you may have a Highway A in nearly every county. Today, more than half of the state highways in Missouri are lettered highways. Missouri and Wisconsin are the only two states to use letters to designate state highways.

31.0 Parts for Planes

If you look to your right you can see a 1960s vintage Lear 23 jet poking through the trees at 30.4. This marks White Industries, one of the largest and oldest suppliers of used airframe, engine, and avionics parts. You might also glimpse the tails of the 2,600 aircraft in their inventory. White acquires 100 to 120 planes per year. Although most are flown in, landing on the 4,400-foot-long runway, others are salvaged from accident scenes and brought by truck. Over the years they have removed planes from such difficult places as a fishing camp on Great Slave Lake, a glacier in Greenland, and an African forest.

30.0 Jackson County

You will soon enter Jackson County, the second most populous county in Missouri, behind St. Louis County. Jackson County was named for U.S. President Andrew Jackson. During the Civil War most of the county was burned to the ground by the Union army as a result of a direct order approved by President Lincoln. This tactic was meant to drive out the Confederate sympathizers. Jackson County figures prominently in the history of the Mormon Church (Church of Jesus Christ of Latter-Day Saints) and the Community of Christ (formerly Reorganized Church of Latter-Day Saints). In 1831, about 2,000 members followed their prophet Joseph Smith Jr. from Ohio to what is now Jackson County. Smith proclaimed the town of Independence to be "Zion"—the city of God. He prophesized that Independence

1960s vintage Lear 23 jet

would be the site of Christ's return and the New Jerusalem. The Mormons were run out of Missouri in 1839 in part because of their antislavery and pro–Native American views. After being expelled from Missouri, leader Joseph Smith Jr. was killed and the church split into factions. One group led by his son Joseph Smith III was called the Reorganized Church of the Latter Day Saints. This group returned to Jackson County and established their headquarters in Independence in the early 1900s. The other group followed Brigham Young to Salt Lake City. You can visit the Mormon Visitor Center and two buildings, the temple and the auditorium. Visitors can listen to recitals and view the temple's 5,685-pipe organ and the auditorium's 6,334-pipe organ.

28.0 Top Cat

High above the horizon on the right, a sign with two pointy ears on a round cat's head alerts the drivers of tractor trailers that a Certified Scales site is ahead. The cartoon-like shape is the logo for the Certified Scales Corporation, the largest truck scale network in the world with over 1,000 locations throughout the United States and Canada. In 1977, this company introduced the first totally automated full-length platform scale. Before that, most scales could not weigh a truck accurately because they could not weigh the truck and trailer together. If truckers fail their weight inspection at the weigh stations they must pay hefty fines. These Certified scales help truckers check the weight of their load before they pass through a weigh station. Regulations for trucks vary from state to state. In Missouri, the maximum weight for semi tractors is 80,000 pounds. Without weight limits roads would deteriorate more quickly and safety could be jeopardized for both truckers and other drivers.

26.0 Leaving Ag Lands

The town of Grain Valley (Exit 24) and Adams's Dairy Farm Road (Exit 21) call attention to the agricultural heritage of this area. For the past 100 miles you have been traveling through agricultural lands. Yet as you look around you see suburban development. As the suburbs of Kansas City expand, agricultural land is being converted and lost to urban uses. These next few miles are the interface between city and country. You are crossing the current border between rural and urban, but in the future this border likely will continue to move east.

24.0 Highway Homes

In the land between city and country, recreational vehicle (RV) dealerships start on the left, but soon you will see them on both sides of the highway. Located on the urban/rural border, these RV dealers offer both the comforts of city conveniences and the thrills of remote country. Like a turtle that carries its home upon its back, RV enthusiasts take their living quarters with them as they travel across the country. The largest and most luxurious motor homes contain washer-dryers, kitchens, televisions, bathrooms, basements, and even hot tubs. In 2007, about 350,000 motor homes nationwide were bought from lots like you see surrounding you. RV owners share a passion for the road and for the comforts of home that they can take along everywhere they go. St. Augustine noted that "the world is a book, and those who do not travel read only a page." RV owners are avid readers of the American landscape.

23.0 What's in a Name?

On the right at 22.4 is Lake Remembrance. Only five years after our country witnessed the heroism of our civil servants on

September 11, the citizens of Blue Springs voted to name this city lake in remembrance of all firefighters, police officers, and military personnel who give their lives to protect ours. (See related mile 147 firefighter's memorial.) While most places were named by the postmaster general or an affluent person in the community for a person they deemed important, this place elicits a warm communal spirit because many voices named it for the memories of all civil servants. Within this nostalgic lake you will also see the Anti-Vortex Intake Velocity Control Structure (a.k.a. That Round Metal Thing in the Water Next to the Highway). This carefully named structure was designed to keep debris out of an intake structure and to keep water from swirling and forming a vortex—hence the name. We hope you enjoyed the stories of other Missouri names as you made memories along the highway today.

20.0 Harley-Davidson

The Blue Springs Harley-Davidson dealership on the left is one of 1,300 dealerships in sixty countries, but Missouri is one of only three states that offers a factory tour that shows how these famous motorcycles evolve from sheets of metal to a finished product. At the factory located in North Kansas City you can even witness them getting a "test run" before being released onto the open road. York, Pennsylvania, and Wauwatosa, Wisconsin, are the only other places where you can see this unique process. While you may have spied a few pigs as you traveled across Missouri, you may have seen a few H.O.G.s, too! Eighty years after William Harley and the Davidson brothers produced the first Harley in 1903, the H.O.G. (Harley Owners Group) formed. Today it has grown to more than one million members. As you journey across the wild Missouri landscape, adopt the H.O.G.'s mission to "Ride and Have Fun."

18.0 Oh, Deer

Watch for deer in suburban environments, such as in the park-like land on the right. Deer numbers have increased significantly since the 1930s when it was rare to see a deer. Because of excessive hunting and habitat changes, in 1930 only about 200 deer were left in Missouri. But deer management has increased the numbers dramatically. In 2006, Missouri hunters killed over

Santa Fe Trail wagon ruts near Kansas City (Kansas City Public Library, Missouri)

200,000 deer and yet approximately 1.4 million deer still roamed Missouri in 2007. Urban deer herds are growing particularly fast because hunting in urban areas is limited for safety reasons. Biologists with the Missouri Department of Conservation report that about 8 percent (112,000 deer) live in urban areas. As you travel across Missouri you will undoubtedly see dead deer lying by the roadside. About 8,000 automobile accidents involving deer occur each year in Missouri.

17.0 Independence: Trails and Truman

Exit 12 will take you to the Truman Presidential Library and Museum and the former home of the 33rd president of the United States, Harry S Truman. That's not a typo. There is no period after the S because it is not an initial but his full middle name, which was given to honor his two grandfathers whose names started with the letter S. President Truman lived here from the age of twenty-two until his death at the age of eighty-eight in 1972. During his presidency it was known as the "Summer White House." Truman was called the "People's President" because of his folksy demeanor, his "buck stops here" philosophy, and his humble roots. Truman made some of the most important decisions in history, including the decision to drop atomic bombs on Japan and the decision to come to the defense of South Korea, which led to U.S. involvement in what would become the Korean War. Truman's birthday is a state holiday in Missouri.

Independence was a jumping-off point for the Santa Fe, Oregon, and California trails. More than a quarter-million people heading west to the "promised land" launched their journeys from Independence. You can visit the National Frontier Trails Museum to learn more about these courageous and ambitious travelers. Wagon ruts from the Santa Fe wagon trains are still visible near the museum. For more information about the Santa Fe Trail in Missouri, refer back to 107W (page 46).

KANSAS CITY, THE CITY OF FOUNTAINS

11.0 Kansas City

Welcome to Kansas City, famous for blues, beef, barbeque, and boulevards. In fact, Kansas Citians claim that only Paris has more boulevards. It is also famous for its fountains, having more than 200. Kansas Citians also claim that only Rome has more fountains. A fountain is the logo for the city, and "City of Fountains" is an official nickname.

Ahead you will see the Truman Sports Complex. This complex includes Kauffman Stadium and Arrowhead Stadium, home of the baseball Royals and football Chiefs, respectively. Arrowhead Stadium is a notoriously difficult place for opposing teams because of the raucous sellout crowds known as the "Red Sea." The noise of the boisterous crowds has been measured at as high as 120 decibels, which is similar to the loudness of a jet taking off. Ahead on the left you will get a great view into Kauffman Stadium. At the east end of I-70 near the Mississippi in downtown St. Louis you saw Busch Stadium, home of the Cardinals. When the Royals and Cardinals played in the 1985 World Series it was called the "I-70 World Series." As you pass the stadiums you will be driving on the George Brett Super Highway. He is in the Baseball Hall of Fame and forever will be a hero of Royals fans.

Away from the Midwest many people assume Kansas City is in Kansas, and in fact there is a Kansas City, Kansas, on the west side of the Kansas River, but it is much smaller than Kansas City, Missouri. Kansas City, Missouri, is the 40th-largest city in the United States with a population of 445,000.

The tallest skyscraper in the skyline ahead is also the tallest building in all of Missouri. One Kansas City Place is an office building that stretches forty-two floors up to 632 feet (651 feet if you include the antenna). Built in 1988, One Kansas City Place exceeds the height of the St. Louis Gateway Arch by 2 feet at its rooftop and by 21 feet at the top of its antenna. You can recognize it ahead by its blue glass walls by day and red, white, and blue lights that shine from the top at night. Throughout the year, the colors change to red for important Chiefs games, blue for important Royals games, red for Valentine's Day, green for St. Patrick's Day, pink for Breast Cancer Awareness Month (October), and red and green for Christmas. The freestanding tower on the left horizon is KCTV's 1,042-foot transmitter tower. It is the tallest freestanding structure in Missouri and the 31st-tallest tower in the world.

Off to the left as you approach the I-670 exit (just past mile 4.0) you will see another island of tall buildings. These buildings are part of Crown Center, a city within a city. Crown Center is named for the crown in the Hallmark logo. One of the nation's first mixed-use urban redevelopments, it was the vision of Joyce C. Hall, founder of Hallmark Cards, and his son, current Hallmark chairman Donald J. Hall. They wanted to replace urban blight with high-quality entertainment and residential and business facilities. It is home to the corporate headquarters of Hallmark Cards, and a visitors center tells the story of the world's largest greeting card company. You will get a closer look at Crown Center on your left as you near downtown. The tallest building you see is the 40-story Hyatt Regency Crown Center, with its revolving rooftop restaurant. For several years it was the tallest building in Kansas City. This is the site of America's worst disaster related to an engineering failure. On July 17, 1981, two walkways in the hotel atrium fell onto hundreds of people attending a fancy tea dance. A total of 114 people were killed, and more than 200 others injured. A design flaw was to blame for this historic tragedy.

Exit 3B places you into the historic 18th and Vine district. This intersection made famous by the lyrics to the oft-recorded blues-rock standard "Kansas City" is now home to the American Jazz Museum, the premier interactive jazz museum in the world. The 18th and Vine neighborhood was home to Charlie

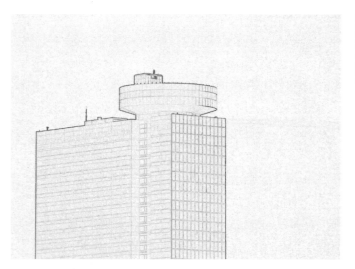

Hyatt Regency Crown Center

Parker, Count Basie, and many other jazz greats of the twenties, thirties, and forties. The museum even has an operating jazz club called the Blue Room. Sharing this intersection is the Negro Baseball League Museum. Major League baseball teams often visit the museum when they are in town. Several U.S. presidents and many celebrities have come to learn about and pay their respects to the Negro baseball players prevented from playing in the major leagues.

In the heart of downtown the City Market Area is visible to your right (Exit 2D). This neighborhood was Kansas City's first commercial district and has open-air markets and trendy lofts and restaurants in what had been abandoned warehouses and office buildings. It is also home to the *Steamship Arabia,* a paddlewheel boat that in 1856 hit a tree stump and quickly sunk into the muddy Missouri. In 1987, it was discovered a half mile from the current river channel and "raised" from 45 feet under a Kansas cornfield. Because it sunk quickly, the 222 tons of freight heading from St. Louis to frontier stores was found to be intact. This made the *Steamship Arabia* an amazing nineteenth-century time capsule. The cargo contained clothes, tools, perfume, and other assorted products of everyday life. These items are on display, making the experience like walking into an 1856

Lewis and Clark at the confluence of the Missouri and Kansas rivers (LuAnn Cadden)

department store. You can even watch as technicians clean, restore, and catalog these items.

FAREWELL

Your journey across Missouri comes to an end here near the junction of the Kansas and Missouri rivers. Lewis and Clark were among the many explorers and settlers that used this riverine superhighway as they headed west. They camped here on their famous expedition in 1804 and again on the return trip in 1806. At the confluence, Clark recorded the Kansas River as being 230 yards wide while the Missouri was 500 yards wide, both much wider at that time than they are today. It is hard to believe, as you look about you, that during their three days exploring this area in 1804, they saw their first buffalo, numerous deer, their first wolf, and a huge flock of the once common and now extinct Carolina parakeets. In Kansas City they marveled at the "verry fine" country that they saw. Clark wrote, on June 25, 1804, "The prairies come within a short distance of the river on each side which contains in addition to Plumbs, Raspberries, and vast quantities of wild (crab) apples . . . and wildflowers, great numbers of deer." Since Lewis and Clark's time, railroad tracks replaced animal tracks, howling sirens replaced howling wolves, airplanes replaced colorful parakeets, and big skyscrapers replaced the big sky.

As you cross the Kansas River consider the words of John Kauffmann who wrote, "Rivers have what man most respects and longs for in his own life and thought—a capacity for renewal and replenishment, continual energy, creativity, cleansing." Our wish is that like the many rivers that you have crossed on your journey you have found renewal and replenishment in the stories of the courage, resourcefulness, productivity, and enterprise of Missourians and inspiration from the beauty of Missouri's forests, fields, and streams. If you, like Lewis and Clark, are continuing your journey west, we wish you smooth sailing and happy trails. Thank you for traveling with us across the Show Me State of Missouri.

Eastbound

COMING FROM KANSAS

The skyline of Kansas City beckons to travelers even when they are still over 10 miles to the west in Kansas. The tallest skyscraper visible in the skyline ahead is also the tallest building in all of Missouri. One Kansas City Place is forty-two floors high, stretching up to 632 feet (651 feet including the antenna). Built in 1988, One Kansas City Place exceeds the height of the St. Louis Gateway Arch by 2 feet at its rooftop and by 21 feet at the top of its antenna. You can recognize it ahead in the daytime by its blue-gray glass walls and at night by the red, white, and blue lights shining from the top of the building. Throughout the year, the colors change to red for important Chiefs games, blue for important Royals games, red for Valentine's Day, green for St. Patrick's Day, pink for Breast Cancer Awareness Month (October), and red and green for Christmas.

To the right of the downtown skyscrapers is KCTV's 1,042-foot-high transmitter tower. It is the tallest freestanding structure in Missouri and the 31st-tallest tower in the world.

Away from the Midwest many people assume Kansas City is in Kansas. There is indeed a Kansas City, Kansas, on the west side of the Kansas River, and in fact you drive through it as you approach Missouri on I-70, but it is much smaller than Kansas City, Missouri. Kansas City, Missouri, is the 40th-largest city in the United States with a population of 445,000.

As you approach the state line you will notice that downtown Kansas City is perched above the surrounding floodplains. Down and to the right from One Kansas City Place, you will see the gold dome of the Cathedral of the Immaculate Conception, which is the seat of the Catholic diocese of Kansas City and St. Joseph, Missouri. One hundred years before One Kansas City Place found its place in the skyline, this cathedral was the tallest building in Kansas City. Known as the oldest worshiping congregation of Kansas City, the forerunner of the cathedral began

78

One Kansas City Place

Cathedral of the Immaculate Conception with One Kansas City Place in background

in a log cabin in 1834. In 1883, early settler François Chouteau funded the cathedral's construction. The 23-carat-gold dome was applied in 1960.

You will cross the Kansas River near its junction with the Missouri River (visible far to the left) and as you do you will enter Missouri. I-70 will roughly parallel the Missouri River all of the way across the state, and you will cross it twice before you reach St. Louis. Lewis and Clark were among the many explorers and settlers that used this riverine superhighway as they headed west. They camped here on their famous expedition in 1804 and again on the return trip in 1806. Clark recorded the Kansas River as being 230 yards wide while the Missouri was 500 yards wide, both much wider at that time than they are today. During their three days exploring this area in 1804, Lewis and Clark saw their first buffalo, numerous deer, their first wolf, and a huge flock of the now-extinct Carolina parakeets. They also marveled at the "verry fine" country here at what is now Kansas City. On June 25, 1804, Clark wrote that "the prairies come within a short distance of the river on each side which contains in addition to Plumbs, Raspberries, and vast quantities of wild (crab) apples . . . and wildflowers, great numbers of deer." Since Lewis and Clark's time, railroad tracks replaced animal tracks, howling sirens replaced howling wolves, airplanes replaced colorful parakeets, and big skyscrapers replaced big sky.

Most travelers driving into Kansas City on I-70 will be directed to take I-670, which runs directly west, rather than the slower I-70 route that winds north of downtown. These two routes quickly join up again 3 miles into Missouri just east of downtown. Regardless of the route taken, after crossing the Kansas River and entering Missouri you can look down on the West Bottoms area that once was home to the bustling Kansas City Stockyards and Livestock Exchange. The railroads below delivered livestock that made Kansas City famous for steaks. Cattle trains no longer arrive because it is cheaper to slaughter and process the cattle near where they are raised and then to transport the meat, rather than to transport live animals here. However, as you can see from these Santa Fe and Union Pacific yards, Kansas City is still a major railroad town.

WELCOME TO KANSAS CITY, CITY OF FOUNTAINS

Welcome to Kansas City, famous for blues, beef, barbeque, and boulevards. In fact, Kansas Citians claim that only Paris

Stockyards, Kansas City (Kansas City Public Library, Missouri)

has more boulevards. It is also famous for its fountains, having more than 200. Kansas Citians also claim that only Rome has more fountains. A fountain is the logo for the city, and "City of Fountains" is an official nickname.

Travelers Entering on I-70

Far to the left you can see the runway of the Charles B. Wheeler Downtown Airport. This airport was the primary city airport until 1972 when the current airport was built 20 minutes north of here. This is still a busy airport, with up to 700 corporate or other private aircraft taking off or landing here each day.

Upon entering downtown, you can see the City Market area on the left (Exit 2D). This was Kansas City's first commercial district. Today this neighborhood of trendy lofts and restaurants continues its market tradition, with over 590,000 people annually visiting the numerous ethnic groceries and largest farmer's market in the Midwest. This market began in 1857 as a place of bartering, horse-trading, political rallies, and medicine shows. The City Market area is also home to the *Steamship Arabia*, a paddlewheel boat that in 1856 hit a tree stump and quickly sank into the muddy Missouri. In 1987, it was discovered a half mile from the current river channel and "raised" from 45 feet under what is now a Kansas cornfield. Because it sank quickly, the 222 tons of freight heading from St. Louis to frontier stores was found intact. This made the *Steamship Arabia* a nineteenth-century time capsule. The cargo contained clothes, tools, perfume, and other assorted products of everyday life. These items are on display, offering an experience that's like walking into an 1856 department store. You can watch as technicians clean, restore, and catalog these items.

Travelers Entering on I-670

The large white building to the right is Kemper Arena. Each year it is home to a famous and historic eight-week-long livestock show called the American Royal (the source of the Kansas City Royals's name), which includes rodeos and the world's biggest barbeque competition. Kemper Arena was the site of the 1976 Republican National Convention.

To the left, as you approach the ridge, you can see a bull rising above the trees on a 90-foot-high tower. This bull had been on the American Hereford Association building. The bull was nicknamed "Bob" ("Bull on Building") and is a symbol of the stockyards and Kansas City's colorful history as a livestock center.

Entering downtown you will drive directly under the Kansas City Convention Center. Its four tall art deco pylons with support cables allow for 388,800 square feet of column-free exhibit space on one floor. Sprint Center, which is on your left, opened in 2007. It occupies 8.5 acres and holds up to 18,000 people for concerts and sporting events.

18th and Vine

Exits 3A and 4B take you into the historic 18th and Vine district. This intersection made famous by the lyrics to the oft-recorded blues-rock standard "Kansas City" is home to the American Jazz Museum, the premier interactive jazz museum in the world. This neighborhood was home to Charlie Parker, Count Basie, and other jazz greats of the twenties, thirties, and forties. The museum has an operating jazz club called the Blue Room. Sharing this intersection is the Negro Baseball League Museum. Major league baseball teams, several U.S. presidents, and many

Bob the Bull

celebrities have come to learn about and pay their respects to the Negro baseball players who were not allowed to play in the major leagues.

Beyond the I-435 interchange, you will see the Truman Sports Complex on the right, which includes Kauffman Stadium and Arrowhead Stadium, home of the baseball Royals and football Chiefs, respectively. Kauffman Stadium blocks the view of Arrowhead, but if you look back over your shoulder you can glimpse it. Arrowhead Stadium is a notoriously difficult place for opposing teams because of the raucous sellout crowds known as the "Red Sea." The noise of the boisterous crowds has been measured at as high as 120 decibels, which is similar to the loudness of a jet taking off. At the east end of I-70 in Missouri just before you cross the Mississippi River you will glimpse the St. Louis Cardinals's stadium. When the Royals and Cardinals played in the 1985 World Series it was called the "I-70 World Series." As you pass Kauffman Stadium, you will be driving on the George Brett Super Highway. He played his entire career as a Kansas City Royal and is in the Baseball Hall of Fame.

FROM KANSAS CITY TO COLUMBIA

As you leave Kansas City, we will now begin to use mile markers to place our stories. For those using this book in your car, please take care that your car's driver keeps his or her eyes on the road. On average, 75,508 vehicles, including almost 13,000 trucks, drive along I-70 in Missouri each day. With this high volume of traffic caution is necessary to avoid an unwanted meeting with your fellow I-70 travelers.

11.0 Independence: Trails and Truman

Exit 12 will take you to the Truman Presidential Library and Museum and the former home of the 33rd president of the United States, Harry S Truman. That's not a typo. There is no period after the S because it is not an initial but his full middle name, which was given to honor his two grandfathers whose names started with the letter S. President Truman lived here from the age of twenty-two until his death at the age of eighty-eight in 1972. During his presidency it was known as the "Summer White House." Truman was called the "People's President" because of his folksy demeanor, his "buck stops here" philosophy, and his humble roots. Truman made some of the most important decisions in history, including the decision to drop atomic bombs on Japan and the decision to come to the defense of South Korea, which led to U.S. involvement in what would become the Korean War. Truman's birthday is a state holiday in Missouri.

Independence was a jumping-off point for the Santa Fe, Oregon, and California trails. More than a quarter-million people heading west to the "promised land" launched their journeys from Independence. You can visit the National Frontier Trails Museum to learn more about these courageous and ambitious travelers. Wagon ruts from the Santa Fe wagon trains are still visible near the museum. For more information about the Santa Fe Trail in Missouri see 107W (page 46).

14.0 Jackson County

You are currently in Jackson County, the second most populous county in Missouri, behind St. Louis County. Jackson County is named for Andrew Jackson, U.S. senator and president from Tennessee. During the Civil War, acting on a direct order approved by President Lincoln, the Union Army burned most of the county to the ground. Jackson County figures prominently in the history of the Mormon Church and the Community of Christ (formerly the Reorganized Church of Jesus Christ of Latter Day Saints). In 1831, about 2,000 members followed their prophet, Joseph Smith Jr., from Ohio to this area. Smith proclaimed the town of Independence to be "Zion"—the city of God—and prophesized that Independence would be the site of Christ's return and the New Jerusalem. But in 1839 the Mormons were run out of Missouri in part because of their antislavery and pro–Native American views. After his expulsion from Missouri, Joseph Smith Jr. was killed and the church split into factions. One group led by his son Joseph Smith III was called the Reorganized Church of Jesus Christ of the Latter Day Saints. This group returned and established their headquarters in Independence. The other group followed Brigham Young to Salt Lake City. You can visit the Mormon Visitor Center and two impressive buildings, the temple and the auditorium. Visitors can listen to regularly scheduled recitals played on the temple's 5,685-pipe organ and the auditorium's 6,334-pipe organ.

17.0   Oh, Deer

Watch for deer in suburban environments, such as in the park-like land on the left. Deer numbers have increased significantly since the 1930s when it was rare to see a deer. Because of excessive hunting and habitat changes, in 1930 only about 200 deer were left in Missouri. But deer management has increased the numbers dramatically. In 2006, Missouri hunters killed over 200,000 deer and yet approximately 1.4 million deer still roamed Missouri in 2007. Urban deer herds are growing particularly fast because hunting in urban areas is limited for safety reasons. Biologists with the Missouri Department of Conservation report that about 8 percent (112,000 deer) live in urban areas. As you travel across Missouri you will undoubtedly see dead deer lying by the roadside. About 8,000 automobile accidents involving deer occur each year in Missouri.

19.0   Harley-Davidson

The Blue Springs Harley-Davidson dealership on the left is one of 1,300 dealerships in sixty countries, but Missouri is one of only three states that offers a factory tour that shows how these famous motorcycles evolve from sheets of metal to a finished product. At the factory located in North Kansas City you can even witness them getting a "test run" before being released onto the open road. York, Pennsylvania, and Wauwatosa, Wisconsin, are the only other places where you can see this unique process. While you may spy a few pigs as you travel across Missouri, you may also see a few H.O.G.s, too! Eighty years after William Harley and the Davidson brothers produced the first Harley in 1903, the H.O.G. (Harley Owners Group) formed. Today it has grown to more than one million members. As you journey across the wild Missouri landscape, adopt the H.O.G.'s mission to "Ride and Have Fun."

20.0 Blue Springs

Directly next to the I-70/Highway 7 ramp on your left, a blue spring rises 25 feet high at the top and 19 feet across. Evening travelers can see the fountain illuminated in refreshing shades of brilliant blue. Artist Brower Hatcher's *Blue Spring,* installed in 2006, reminds passersby that this large metropolitan area once began as a town settled at the site where a crystal blue spring flowed into the Little Blue River. Over the years the Little Blue region has become swamped by civilization. Fortunately, the namesake of this growing metropolis will not be forgotten, thanks to this landmark and the caring citizens who organize river cleanups and civic activities to remind residents of Blue Springs's origin.

21.0 Entering Ag Lands

Adams's Dairy Farm Road (Exit 21) and the town of Grain Valley (Exit 24) call attention to the area's agricultural heritage. As the suburbs of Kansas City expand, more and more agricultural land is converted to urban uses. These next few miles are the interface between city and country. You are crossing the current border between urban and rural, but this border will continue to move east as the suburbs grow. Beyond Grain Valley for the next 100 miles you will be traveling through farmland. You will see mostly hay or grain crop production. The hay crop will be brome grass. Pastures of this nonnative grass are mowed two or three times each growing season. The hay is then baled

Blue Spring

and moved to a barn or feedlot. The grain crops include corn, sorghum, and wheat. Corn and sorghum are grass crops with long wide leaves on a single stalk. Corn grows 8 to 10 feet tall with ears on the stalk. Sorghum, also called "milo," typically is shorter and starts to produce a grain head at the top when it is about 10 inches tall. Wheat blankets the entire field instead of being in rows. Winter wheat is planted in the fall. It sprouts and creates a bright green cover that becomes dormant in the winter. In the spring it grows again and changes to a golden color for harvest time in summer.

23.0   Highway Homes

In the land between city and country, recreational vehicle (RV) dealerships start on the left, but soon you will see them on both sides of the highway. Located on the urban/rural border, these RV dealers offer both the comforts of city conveniences and the thrills of remote country. Like a turtle that carries its home upon its back, RV enthusiasts take their living quarters with them as they travel across the country. The largest and most luxurious motor homes contain washer-dryers, kitchens, televisions, bathrooms, basements, and even hot tubs. In 2007, about 350,000 motor homes nationwide were bought from lots like you see surrounding you. RV owners share a passion for the road and for the comforts of home that they can take along everywhere they go. St. Augustine noted that "the world is a book, and those who do not travel read only a page." RV owners are avid readers of the American landscape.

24.0 Wetlands, Not Wastelands

Ahead on the right you can see a type of wetland called a "bottomland" (or riparian) forest. In spring and early summer, water will be standing in the woods, but wetlands are not necessarily always wet. River bottom trees include pin oak, cottonwood, elm, ash, willow, river birch, silver maple, sycamore, hackberry, and sweetgum. Wetlands benefit people in many ways and they are more valuable than most people realize. Water in tree-lined streams is, on average, 10 degrees cooler than nonforested streams. A healthy stream depends on a healthy forest growing on its banks, and tree-lined riverbanks significantly lessen the impact of flooding by serving as a giant sponge to soak up water and slow fast-flowing floodwaters. Wonderful wetlands are nature's filters as they purify the water by removing sediments and chemicals. They also replenish the groundwater, protect shorelines, and hold soil in place to help prevent erosion. Sometimes they serve as nurseries for young fish. Wetlands are also home to many interesting and useful plants and animals, including wood ducks and other waterfowl that migrate across North America, as well as several endangered species. Wetlands provide recreation opportunities such as birdwatching, fishing, photography, and canoeing, along with enhancing the scenic beauty of an area. And yet because of conversion to other uses, only 20 percent of Missouri's original 4 million acres of bottomland forests remain.

27.0 Top Cat

High above the horizon on the right, a sign with two pointy ears on a round cat's head alerts the drivers of tractor trailers that a Certified Scales site is ahead. The cartoon-like shape is the logo for the Certified Scales Corporation, the largest truck scale network in the world with over 1,000 locations throughout the United States and Canada. In 1977, this company introduced the first totally automated full-length platform scale. Before that, most scales could not weigh a truck accurately because they could not weigh the truck and trailer together. If truckers fail their weight inspection at the weigh stations they must pay hefty fines. These Certified scales help truckers check the weight of their load before they pass through a weigh station. Regulations for trucks vary from state to state. In Missouri, the maximum weight for semi tractors is 80,000 pounds. Without weight limits roads would deteriorate more quickly and safety could be jeopardized for both truckers and other drivers.

30.0 Parts for Planes

If you look quickly to your left, you can see a 1960s vintage Lear 23 jet poking through the trees. This marks White Industries, one of the largest and oldest suppliers of used airframe, engine, and avionics parts. You might also glimpse the tails of the 2,600 aircraft in their inventory. White acquires 100 to 120 planes per year. Although most are flown in, landing on the 4,400-foot-long runway, others are salvaged from accident scenes and brought by truck. Over the years they have removed planes from such difficult places as a fishing camp on Great Slave Lake, a glacier in Greenland, and an African forest.

31.0 "La Fayette, We Are Here."

You have just entered Lafayette County, named after Marie-Joseph Paul Yves Roch Gilbert du Motier. Yes, that is the name of just one person, a man also known as the Marquis de La Fayette. It is a good thing he had this title because his full name would not fit on the historical markers and other city signs honoring this defender of liberty. La Fayette joined the French army at fourteen years old. As a nineteen-year-old officer, against the warnings of his friends and even Benjamin Franklin, then the U.S. envoy to France, La Fayette risked his life to come to America to fight in the Revolutionary War. The British sent two ships to capture him, but he escaped using a disguise. After a two-month journey he landed safely in South Carolina. Upon arrival, this teenage officer received an honorary rank of major general in the American army. He refused his salary and led his men to battle as a volunteer. He became a lifelong friend of George Washington and named a son after him. After the war, La Fayette returned to France and played a prominent and colorful role in French history during the French Revolution. During World War II, when General Patton visited La Fayette's grave in France, he said, "La Fayette, we are here"—a reference to the U.S. army repaying the debt owed to La Fayette for his service to America. In 2002, President George W. Bush made La Fayette an honorary U.S. citizen.

33.0 Wrong Way Creek

As you cross over the Sni-a-bar (pronounced SNEYE-uh-bahr) Creek, be grateful for well-marked highways and detailed road maps. Sni-a-bar Creek was once a tricky waterway that fooled at least one trapper to steer off the Missouri River and travel quite a distance before he realized his mistake. In an account of Stephen Harriman Long's expedition to the Rocky Mountains in 1823, we learn the story about the lost trapper named "Barre" and the tricky "Cheny au Barre" (note the phonetic similarity) that misled him. "Sni" seems to have come from variations of "channel," which is *chenal* in French, and "bar" seems to come from the trapper's name. You don't have to worry about taking a wrong turn on the well-marked I-70.

34.0 Ritchie Brothers Auction

Ritchie Brothers Truck Auction ahead on the right is just one of 110 locations in 25 countries. Ritchie Brothers is the world's largest auctioneer of industrial equipment, employing almost 1,000 full-time employees. The company sells, through public auctions, used and new industrial equipment from the construction, transportation, marine, mining, forestry, petroleum, real estate, and agricultural industries. It was established in 1958 in British Columbia, Canada. You may see bulldozers, cement mixers, or cranes for sale here. In 2007, they held 350 auctions with gross proceeds of more than $3 billion.

35.0 Odessa

Ahead is the town of Odessa. In 1880 the townspeople of Kirkpatrick were searching for a new town name because founder John Kirkpatrick did not want to risk attaching his name to a town he thought would fail. T. B. Blackstone, president of the Chicago & Alton Railroad, noticed the area's gentle hills and told the people how these rolling wheat fields reminded him of the city Odessa in the Ukraine. His inspiration gave the town a new name. If today Kirkpatrick could see this thriving community of over 9,000 people, perhaps he would regret removing his name from a town that did not fail after all. If you are traveling during the first full weekend of August you can stop for the annual Puddle Jumper Days festival. This fun event celebrates a train called a "puddle jumper," which made stops between Odessa and nearby towns in the early 1900s. A puddle jumper (also called a "doodlebug") was a self-propelled passenger-carrying railcar. Most were built in the 1910s and 1920s. The last ones quit running around 1960.

37.0 Lake Venita

On the right as you go up the hill, you can glimpse Lake Venita, a humble little remnant of a popular resort between Kansas City and St. Louis in the "roaring 1920s." Originally dedicated as Mulvill Lake on April 3, 1908, it was renamed "Venita" for John Kirkpatrick's niece. Cottages, boats, a beach, and a dancing pavilion provided a place to relax along the water by day and dance by night. Today, Dyer Park still provides pleasure for the people of Odessa. Locals and travelers enjoy fishing, baseball, a children's playground, and an annual rodeo. Even though the cabins have been gone for over thirty years, travelers can spend the evening in tents while dancing music still echoes through the night—although square dancing (Missouri's state dance) has replaced the Charleston.

38.0 Don't Treat Soil Like Dirt

As you drive, look around at the productive farmland. It is productive because of its soil. Agronomists study soil and take it seriously. To them, what you see on the fields is not dirt; it's soil. Dirt is what's under your bed or fingernails. Soil is a mixture of tiny particles worn from rocks, dead plants and animals (called organic matter), water, air, and tiny living organisms called "decomposers." Decomposers convert organic matter into nutrients that can be taken up again and used by plants. Good soil grows healthy crops, animals, and people. Our soil is a national treasure. Franklin D. Roosevelt said, "The nation that destroys its soil, destroys itself." Without rich soil our nation would be "dirt poor."

39.0 Family Farm

From 1959 to 2000 the pretty Ridgewood Farm on the left was a dairy farm featuring award-winning red-and-white Holsteins, instead of the more common black-and-white variety. Dairy cattle from this farm were exported to Europe, Japan, and South America. In 1967, this farm produced a Grand Champion at the World Dairy Expo. The milking operation was shut down in 2000 when it became too expensive and time-consuming. Today Ron (who grew up on the farm) and Lisa Williams have 1,400 acres of corn, soybeans, and wheat and 120 head of beef cattle.

41.0 Fast Track

The I-70 Race Track at Exit 41 is known as the "Fastest Weekly Short Track in the World." This track hosts races in six classes with cars reaching speeds of 140 mph—twice your speed limit on I-70. The curves on this half-mile oval have steep 30-degree banks, which makes it difficult to stand or walk on them but easier to drive at high speed. Famous NASCAR drivers such as Rusty Wallace, Jeff Gordon, Kenny Schrader, Tony Stewart, and the late Adam Petty have raced here. In fact this is where Adam Petty won his first race. If you have the need for speed, rather than speeding down I-70, you can take a spin on the raceway, either with a driver or by driving yourself.

42.0 Weigh Station

The odd-looking poles that hang over the road ahead signal a weigh station or "chicken coop" as truckers call them. These poles send a signal to a box in their front window that lets truckers know whether they can pass through or if they must stop for an inspection. The first pole turns the box on, the second lets them know whether they have to stop, and the last pole next to the weigh station turns the box off. The Missouri Department of Revenue requires all commercial motor vehicles licensed for 18,000 pounds or more to stop at weigh stations unless directed otherwise. These stations not only check the truck weight but also whether fuel taxes have been paid, if cargo is properly balanced, and if the driver is in proper condition for driving.

44.0 Tall Tank

The blue water tower on the left belongs to Public Water Supply District No. 2. It stores 100,000 gallons of water, 135 feet above the ground. The water stored here is pumped from Higginsville City Lake about 10 miles away. When the lake is low, supplemental water is pumped from the Missouri River, 15 miles north of Higginsville. The water from this tank goes under I-70 to serve 300 to 400 people living south of the interstate. The district rents the top of the tank to ATT/Sprint as a cell phone tower. If you are talking on the phone as you drive down I-70, your voice may be transmitted from the top of this water tank.

45.0 Highway to History

Exit 49 ahead takes you to the Battle of Lexington State Historic Site. A Union army of 2,700 men occupied the pro-Southern town of Lexington. They were attacked by 10,000 Confederate soldiers and proslavery locals in what became known as the Battle of the Hemp Bales. On the way to the battlefield you will pass the road to the Confederate Memorial State Historic Site. For more information about this retirement home for Confederate army veterans and the Battle of Lexington see 52W.

46.0 The Ultimate Sacrifice

The cross ahead on the right at 46.8 honors Trooper Mike Newton, who was killed in an accident here in 2003 at the age of twenty-five. Trooper Newton had stopped a vehicle on the shoulder. While Trooper Newton and the person he had stopped were sitting in his patrol car, they were struck by a pickup whose driver was reaching for a pair of sunglasses. The force of the rear impact caused the patrol car's gas tank to explode and engulf the car in flames. Witnesses pulled the person in the vehicle with Trooper Newton from the patrol car, but they were unable to break the window to get Trooper Newton out of the burning car before ammunition in the car started exploding. Since this tragic crash occurred, the person Trooper Newton pulled over has recovered from severe burns over 40 percent of his body to become an advocate for traffic safety, making appearances throughout Missouri asking drivers to obey the law that requires drivers to "Move Over and Slow Down" when they approach an emergency vehicle.

48.0 Fiber-Optics Fish Farm

The pretty, pastoral, white-fenced farm on the right is not a farm at all. It is the headquarters for Thurman Stout, Inc. d/b/a Ram, a company that lays fiber-optic lines. But until a few years ago it was a fish farm. People paid to fish in the twenty-acre lake and three other smaller ponds on the seventy-four-acre property. The wife of the previous owner was a colorful character known for the speed at which she could clean a fish, and she even won awards for fish cleaning. She also was notorious for catching fish poachers and holding them at gunpoint until they worked off the theft. The ponds are still stocked for the fishing fun of Thurman Stout's employees. The fence surrounding the property is 10,000 feet in length—almost two miles of fencing!

49.0 Man's Best Friend

Sixteen miles south is Warrensburg. It was here where the popular phrase "Man's Best Friend" originated, based on a dearly loved dog named Old Drum, which belonged to Charles Burden. After dogs had killed some of his sheep, a man named Leonidas Hornsby vowed to kill the next dog on his property—and the next one happened to be Old Drum. Burden took Hornsby to trial for killing his dog. The *Burden vs. Hornsby* trial took place on September 23, 1870. Attorney George G. Vest delivered a stirring "Eulogy of the Dog" that swayed every dog owner in the jury to award Burden $50 for damages. In his passionate speech about the unwavering faithfulness of a dog, Vest said, "The one absolutely unselfish friend that a man can have in this selfish world, the one that never deserts him, the one that never proves ungrateful or treacherous, is the dog." His tale became known nationally, and dog lovers from around the country contributed money for a memorial. Old Drum will never be forgotten in Warrensburg as he stands as a full-size bronze statue on the Johnson County Courthouse lawn.

51.0 Microwave Tower

The huge tower on the right is an obsolete ATT microwave communications tower. It was part of a nationwide network of such towers that handled long-distance phone calls. The brick building was built to withstand severe storms or sabotage. It contained equipment that allowed you to call people all over the country as your call was sent from tower to tower. Communication satellites and fiber-optic cables have made the tower obsolete. In fact, three fiber-optic communication cables run from Kansas City to St. Louis within the I-70 right-of-way: one along the north edge, one along the south edge, and one right down the middle. Cars are not the only things speeding along this stretch of highway—information and messages are too. This is a real information highway!

52.0 Aullville

Aullville is named after the Aull brothers. The brothers formed the J. & R. Aull Company, and between 1822 and 1836 John, James, and Robert Aull outfitted pioneers with goods as they traveled west. If they were still in business you could stop at their general store for some coffee, a sunbonnet, stick candy, a cloth doll, or tools in case your wagon (or station wagon) had a breakdown. General stores were sometimes the only businesses in a town and the storekeeper could double as banker and mailman. Many people would barter for their goods or promise to repay debts as they traveled west, but unfortunately time lapses between shipments of goods from the east and debtors not repaying their loans caused the Aull Company to go bankrupt in 1836.

53.0 America's Main Street

Before there were interstates, two-lane federal highways carried people cross-country. The road that you see immediately to the right is old U.S. Route 40. During the heyday of automobile travel in the 1950s it stretched 3,220 miles between Atlantic City and San Francisco and carried more traffic than any other transcontinental highway. It is now about one-third shorter as it ends in Utah. Although U.S. 40 now shares the pavement with I-70 in places, it is still a significant highway in its own right in many stretches along its route. The eastern portion of what eventually became U.S. 40 was part of the National Road, the first federally funded interstate road, begun in 1811, long before the automobile. Between 1926 and 1964, U.S. 40 brought millions of people from the East out into the Great Plains and mountain states. Because so many towns sprang up along U.S. 40 it has been called "America's Main Street." Old U.S. 40 nestles up against

Old gas station along U.S. 40

the south side of I-70 as a frontage road for much of the way across Missouri. You will see abandoned gas stations (such as an abandoned one-pump station at mile 150 ahead on the north side, and King Gas and Diesel just north of Exit 183 where the sign still stands—a sign incapable of giving a gasoline price of more than 99 cents per gallon) and family-owned motels, some still surviving, that sprung up and thrived along America's Main Street.

55.0 Beautiful Barns

As you travel across Missouri you will see dozens of barns such as the white one in the trees on the left. Family farms needed a building where they could house and care for livestock and store grain and equipment. Barn designs for these family farms evolved with a high roof in the center to provide a loft for storing hay and sheds on each side. Many barns had a Gambrel roof, recognized by two ridges added parallel to the center gable ridge, making a steep slope down below the flatter upper slope. This design created a high open loft to store hay. Under haylofts, wagons could be pulled inside and unloaded. Shed attachments on the sides might include workhorse stalls, a small animal pen for baby animals, a shed dedicated to stanchions for eight to twelve milk cows, and a feed room. The silver turrets on the roof are ventilators designed with flues to supply fresh air to the dairy cows. A farmstead may have included a chicken house, storage shed, silo, and grain storage bins. But the barn was the focus for the farm "factory," which took the raw materials from the fields and turned them into dairy products, meat, and other foods.

56.0 Concordia

Ahead you can see the white water tower of Concordia. German immigrants founded this town in 1860. Concordia means "harmony," but its early days were anything but harmonious. On October 10, 1864, bushwhackers killed twenty-five men from Concordia. Bushwhackers were ragtag renegade groups of men with Southern sympathies who roamed the countryside looting and burning farms and villages. Most German citizens opposed slavery and so were targeted by the bushwhackers. As William Quantrill's group of guerrillas neared Concordia, a group of townspeople rode out to meet them (near mile 62 in present-day Emma). Here nearly all the men from Concordia lost their lives and four more were killed in their homes.

57.0 Local Lutheran Heritage

Ahead just past the rest stop and Exit 58 on your right you'll see the campus of St. Paul Lutheran High School, the second oldest Lutheran high school in America, and St. Paul Lutheran Cemetery, where some victims of the Concordia massacre were buried. In 1883, Lutheran pioneers established a college to prepare young men as pastors and teachers who could minister to settlers throughout the West. Today the fifty-acre campus still resembles a college rather than a high school as it is the only Lutheran Church Missouri Synod school to have boarding for students. Of the 200 students who attend St. Paul, one-third are from other countries.

Adjacent to I-70 on the right is a cemetery with nine tombstones that read "October 10, 1864," the date of the massacre described at mile 56. Fifteen Civil War soldiers also are buried here. In what was once a quiet, remote field where St. Paul Lutheran Church members have been laid to rest since 1842, this location today is surrounded by busy twenty-first-century activity. To the

St. Paul Lutheran High School

thousands of busy travelers passing by daily, cemeteries provide an opportunity, as Benedict said, to "day by day remind yourself that you are going to die." Not a morbid thought, but rather, a call to live, love, and forgive more fully today.

59.0 Silos

Tall silos such as these on both sides of I-70 are part of the skyline throughout cattle country. These tall cylindrical structures store feed for cattle. They vary in height from 30 to 100 feet and from 20 to 40 feet in diameter. Silos are filled in late summer and fall with feed for cattle to eat during the winter. Different crops are stored. In fall, corn or a grain sorghum that has partially dried stalks may be chopped into fodder (a coarse feed). When placed in a silo, this fodder ensiles or cures into traditional silage. Silos may also be filled with high-moisture corn that has been harvested early in the fall. Chopped grass crops are cut from fields and when packed in airtight silos the grass cures somewhat like sauerkraut to become haylage, a delectable cattle feed. You will see two kinds of silos along I-70: gray concrete silos and dark blue steel silos. Gray concrete silos often have a silver-colored aluminum dome top. Concrete silos are unloaded from a mechanism at the top that throws the feed down a chute along the side of the silo to wagons or conveyors. The domed top covers the unloader. The feed this type of unloader takes out first is the very last feed that was put in. The deep blue steel silos are called by their trade name "Harvestore." Unlike cement silos these glass-lined steel silos are filled from the top. Harvestores have nearly flat roofs because they are unloaded from the bottom, so they do not need to cover an unloader at the top. Harvestores use bottom unloaders so the first grain loaded is the first taken out.

61.0   St. John Cemetery

To the left, amid the corn at 61.2, you will see a white iron archway that frames the road that leads back to St. John Cemetery, where eight more victims of the Quantrill massacre are buried. The local United Church of Christ was founded on this land in 1850, and the first burial was in 1853. The names on the tombstones, both old and new, reflect the area's German heritage. Beneath the moss on several of the aging stones are German inscriptions and engravings of weeping willows, hands pointing to heaven, and the crown of life.

St. John Cemetery

62.0   Emma

The town with the quaint name of Emma was named for the daughter of the original postmaster, a Reverend Demetrio, who was also the pastor of Holy Cross Lutheran Church. In 1880, no other Missouri town was named Emma so the postmaster general approved it. The U.S. Postal Service controlled the names of new post offices and hence determined the official names of most new towns.

63.0   Disappearing Barns

On the right you will see two old barns. Strong barn construction makes them difficult to tear down. Since space is abundant here in the country, farmers let time and the elements take them down. Large modern tractors and combines no longer fit through the doors, old dirt floors are not hygienic enough for modern milking operations, and enormous round bales of hay no longer need a loft. Although many farm families have a sentimental attachment to their old wooden barns, such barns do not earn any money for the farmer so they fall into neglect, particularly in this day of big corporations taking over small family farms. And few craftsmen exist that know how to fix a barn, even if the owner wanted to save it. Some people encourage conversion of barns into artist studios or bed-and-breakfasts. Others believe these are just different ways of destroying an old barn. Organizations are popping up all over the country to save barns. *Successful Farming* magazine and the National Trust for Historic Preservation have a program called "Barn Again!" This program helps farmers rehabilitate their historic barns and put them back into productive use. Enjoy these beautiful and functional buildings while you can.

65.0   Salt Water in Missouri

A few miles back you entered Saline County, named for the salty springs in the area. The town of Sweet Springs is named for nearby springs that are not salty. Settlers often referred to water that was good-tasting and not salty as being "sweet." When Lewis and Clark passed nearby Salt Creek they noted, "So many licks and salt springs on its banks that the water of the creek is brackish. . . . one bushel of the water is said to make 7 pounds of good salt." The name "licks" comes from the fact that herds of elk, deer, bison, and other animals came to lick the salt. Wolves, mountain lions, bears, and humans came to hunt the animals attracted by the salt, making licks important hunting grounds for predators and humans.

66.0   Highway Hawks

As you drive along you will see large hawks sitting on trees or fences along the highway. Most will be red-tailed hawks. They are common year-round wherever there are trees. Red-tails are attracted to the highway because the grassy medians and rights-of-way provide ideal habitats for their favorite food—mice and other small mammals. Although some people call them "chicken hawks," they do not bother chickens. In fact, red-tailed hawks are valuable to farmers because they eat rodents that in turn would eat the farmers' grain. Look for a mostly white breast with a belly band of variable brown streaks and a short, fan-shaped tail that may be brown or rusty red, depending on the age of the bird.

67.0   Fertile Fields

In some areas the fertile topsoil has been washed away so less productive soil that was covered for centuries is now at the surface. The remaining nutrients in this poorer soil are taken up by plant roots and converted into the standing crops. Whenever crops are harvested, the nutrients, now in the form of plant material, leave the fields by the truckloads. Most farmers turn to chemical fertilizers to replace the nutrients that are lost each year. You may see chemical tanks (often white tanks filled with ammonia) being pulled by tractors or parked by farmsteads. However, applying too much fertilizer can pollute groundwater used for drinking. Fortunately, farmers are developing better techniques that maintain soil fertility for future farmers while still producing a bountiful crop today. One strategy is to leave the dead plant residue from the previous season on the field to hold the soil and to partially reestablish the natural cycle of decaying plant matter going back into the soil. This "no-till" agriculture not only helps hold the rich topsoil in place, but also puts nutrients back in the soil naturally. Look for this crop stubble left in the fields during fall and winter.

69.0 Silent No More

The next 54 miles of I-70 is dedicated to those who have served in the "Silent Service"— submarine veterans. Why 54 miles? This length represents one mile for each of the fifty-two submarines lost in World War II and one mile each for the USS *Thresher* and USS *Scorpion* lost during the Cold War. Submarine veterans hope to have the entire length of I-70 from Maryland to Utah designated as the Submarine Veterans Memorial Highway. See 70W (page 56) for the story of the lone chimney ahead on the left at 70.6.

70.0 EEK!

There is nothing to fear in Houstonia, even though the state highways of EE and K seem to scream EEK! on the next exit sign. You may have already crinkled your brow at these lettered highways and then wondered if you hadn't already passed these two highways before. (You've already passed Highways E and KK.) Even lifelong residents of Missouri have lost bets as to whether these alphabet highways were state or county roads. Because these names are repeated in different counties for entirely different roads, you'd think these narrow two-lane highways must be county roads. But these "farm-to-market" highways are owned and maintained by the Missouri Department of Transportation. In 1952, a gasoline tax allowed the state to connect the rural communities with other towns and to put a state-maintained road within 2 miles of more than 95 percent of all rural family units. Twelve thousand miles of county roads suddenly gained state status and an alphabet name. The problem is that the alphabet just can't cover the entire state. The letters G, I, Q, S, and X are not used because they can be confused with similar letters. So, you may have a Highway A in nearly every county. Today, more than half of the state highways in Missouri are lettered highways. Missouri and Wisconsin are the only two states to use letters to designate state highways.

72.0 Corn Country

Over the next few miles you can see cornfields on the right. Corn is America's number one crop. Corn leads all crops in acreage planted, bushels harvested, and dollar value. In 2006, Missouri growers harvested over 2.6 million acres of corn, producing 363 million bushels, with a value of more than $1.1 billion to this state's economy. Missouri is ranked ninth nationally in corn production. Corn is a North American grain. Europe knew nothing about corn before Columbus discovered it in Cuba in 1492 and took back samples. Native Americans raised corn with red, blue, pink, and black kernels as well as the familiar yellow kernels. But sweet corn that we like to eat directly off the cob was not developed until the 1700s. An ear of corn has about 800 kernels in sixteen rows. A bushel of corn has 72,800 kernels. About 60 percent of the U.S. corn crop is fed to livestock. A bushel of corn fed to livestock produces 5.6 pounds of retail beef, 13 pounds of pork, 20 pounds of chicken, or 28 pounds of catfish. A bushel also can yield 32 pounds of cornstarch, 2.8 gallons of ethanol fuel, or 33 pounds of corn syrup—enough to sweeten more than 400 cans of soda. The average American consumes three pounds of corn every day through food and nonfood uses. More than 4,200 supermarket products contain corn or corn by-products, including such unlikely items as toothpaste, salad dressings, chewing gum, peanut butter, aspirin, catsup, mustard, coffee, and tea. Nonfood items made from corn include detergents, sandpaper, plastics, cosmetics, wallpaper, crayons, shoe polish, ink, fireworks, road deicers, and tires. You may be driving on a corn product right now! To learn about a special Missouri corn product see 75W (page 55).

76.0 Rock Cut

The limestone layers that you pass in the roadside rock cuts are mostly remains of sea animals that died and fell to the bottom of a warm shallow sea. As you speed past this wall of sea creatures you are passing stories in the stones and fascinating finds. Uniform circles on a rock could be the roots of a prehistoric plant. Ancient coral leaves a pattern that looks like a honeycomb. A white spot with wavy edges could reveal shark teeth, and a small cylindrical piece with a hole in the middle could be a stem of a crinoid, Missouri's state fossil. Crinoids, also known as "sea lilies" or "feather-stars," are marine animals that still exist in oceans. Rock cuts are time machines. The past is revealed in many rock cuts over the next 40 miles.

77.0 Road Rock

The quarry on the left is one of more than 900 quarries world-wide owned by the LaFarge Corporation. Twice each month explosives blast the limestone layers mentioned in the previous story into small pieces. Between 2,000 to 3,000 tons of rock per day and more than 500,000 tons of rock each year are removed from the quarry. Most of it is spread on rural roads within 40 miles of the quarry.

79.0 Plethora of Poultry

The long buildings on the left are part of Chris and Heidi Rogers's poultry farm. At any one time 150,000 broilers are being raised here. Chicks arrive by the truckload when they are only three hours old. They must be hand-fed for the first four days. When they are eight weeks old they get shipped to the Tyson plant in Sedalia, Missouri. There are no such things as holidays for the hardworking Rogers family as the chickens require daily care. Their greatest challenge is keeping the chicks alive in extreme summer heat and frigid winter cold.

80.0 The Big Bales

Across central Missouri you will see big round bales rolled up in the fields or stacked near a farmstead. They are hay bales that will feed cattle in winter. They can weigh a ton! Most do actually weigh at least 2,000 pounds. Until the invention of the baler in 1968, hay was gathered loose and pitched to the cattle with a fork. Crews went from farm to farm to compact hay into 60-pound bales, thus making it easier to stack and transport. But handling those bales required a lot of backbreaking labor and the compacting plunger injured many farmers. Today there is an entire industry associated with making and selling balers and associated equipment that has eliminated tedious, difficult hand labor, making it possible for fewer farm workers to supply our food at lower cost.

82.0 Another "Best Friend"

Your route along I-70 is mostly lined by fields and farms, but Missouri's early explorers traveled mostly through trees. Forests such as you see just ahead once covered 70 percent of the state. Clearing for agriculture and supplying wood for transportation needs drastically reduced Missouri's early forests. Missouri forests were first used for fuel for steam-driven riverboats, then they produced thousands of railroad ties for the first railroads, and then they fueled the steam engines that rode those rails. In the early 1900s, 70 acres of forest were cleared each day just to keep Missouri's largest sawmill in business. Today Missouri's 14 million acres of forests cover only about one-third of the state, but Missouri's forest products industry is thriving. Harvesting and processing trees into wood products provide jobs for over 33,000 Missourians working in 2,500 firms (including 417 sawmills), and they contribute over $3 billion each year to Missouri's economy. Missouri's forests still produce railroad ties and lumber, but today Missouri wood products include oak and walnut veneer, tool handles, gunstocks, fence posts, pallets, furniture and cabinets, and Christmas trees. Missouri is a national leader in producing charcoal, barrels, walnut nutmeats, shell products, and redcedar gift items. Forests provide your morning newspaper, your road maps, and the paper for this book. Each year the average American uses the equivalent of one large tree about 100 feet tall and 18 inches in diameter for their wood and paper needs. Back at mile 49 we stated that dogs are man's best friend, but Frank Lloyd Wright stated, "The best friend on earth of man is the tree. When we use the tree respectfully and economically, we have one of the greatest resources on earth."

85.0 Roadside Wildflowers

Ralph Waldo Emerson said, "The earth laughs in flowers." Notice how during summer the rights-of-way laugh in wildflowers. In summer you will likely see the light blue flowers of chicory. Chicory roots were used to make a coffee substitute during World War II and are still used in some trendy coffees. The white flowers are Queen Anne's lace, named because the cluster of small flowers gives a lace-like appearance, complete with a dark red flower where the queen pricked her finger while sewing. It is also called wild carrot because it is a member of the carrot family and the root smells like a carrot. Yellow flowers here are mostly black-eyed Susans. A tea made from black-eyed Susans was used as a folk medicine and a yellow dye can be made from it. In the fall you may see purple-colored asters and the brilliant yellow goldenrod—a plant falsely accused of causing hay fever.

86.0 Smooth Sumac

Over the next two miles you will notice patches of smooth sumac on the hillside to the left. You'll recognize these tree-like shrubs by their long, skinny leaflets that droop like palm leaves. Hillsides are perfect places for sumacs because their extensive root system prevents erosion. By mid-July, sumac has produced its dark red velvety fruits that are a treat for at least thirty-two species of birds. When mixed with sugar and water, the crushed fruit also produces a surprisingly refreshing drink. Native Americans used the fruits to treat fever, the leaves to smoke, and the entire plant for staining and dyeing. While most people don't notice sumac much in the summer, they can't help but see it in the fall. When the green leaves turn to a deep scarlet red, the sumac is the first "tree" to signal that fall has arrived.

87.0 Cell Tower Cluster

This "grove" of cell phone towers is one of several clusters at high points along I-70. Cell towers are recent additions to the landscape. During the 1990s about 5,000 towers were erected per year. Between 2000 and 2002 towers registered with the FCC (a small fraction of all towers) increased from 69,000 to 138,000. New towers continue to pop up like weeds all over the landscape. The convenience of having a cell phone comes at a cost greater than your cell phone bill. Between 5 million and 50 million birds are killed annually by colliding with communication towers in fog or darkness. The FAA requires lights for airplane safety on towers more than 199 feet tall. These lights attract migrating birds. Recommendations to reduce bird kills include placing towers in clusters, such as you see here, or, better yet, encourage firms to share towers, using designs without guy wires (these supporting wires take a huge toll as birds circle the tower lights), avoiding fog-prone areas and migration corridors when building a tower, and eliminating lights on towers less than 200 feet tall. When lights must be put on towers, white strobe lights are best because they don't attract birds as red lights do.

89.0 Fire and Ice

On the right at 89.4 you can catch your first glimpse of the Ozarks. For the next few miles you will get picturesque views of fertile valleys and forested hills where the prairie meets the Ozarks. North of the Missouri River ice formed the land, whereas fire formed the rocky lands to the south. The fertile plains north of the river were scoured by glaciers and left with windblown loess (pronounced "luss") soil. To the south of I-70 volcanic mountains lifted up the plains and then water shaped the valleys and hills that give this land its signature beauty. One ramification of this Ozark terrain is that you will see more pastures for grazing cattle rather than cropland. It is too difficult to cultivate crops in the thin rocky Ozark soil.

90.0 On the Curve

Another effect of the topography is that it forces I-70 to take a wide, sweeping curve after going nearly straight for 90 miles. Such curves are generally unnecessary as I-70 crosses Missouri, but this curve was the only way to avoid having to build six expensive bridges in the next eight miles. The curve takes you south a mile to keep away from the meandering Lamine River. Missouri, whose tourism motto is, "Where the Rivers Run," has fifty-five major river bridges—the most of any state.

91.0 It's All Downhill

As you cross the river floodplain ahead, you are at the lowest point of the trip so far. The elevation has dropped from 760 feet above sea level at the state line in Kansas City to 524 feet at this point. Although the highway has many ups and downs between here and St. Louis, mostly you will be going downhill as St. Louis is only 400 feet above sea level at the edge of the Mississippi River.

92.0 Get the Lead Out

The Lamine River ahead is a tributary of the Missouri River. Daniel Boone trapped and hunted along its banks. In fact, according to Samuel Cole, an early resident, the last hunting and trapping expedition Boone took before he died was to the Lamine River. The name "Lamine" may have come from French explorer Sieur de Bourgmond, who wrote in 1714 that "Indians take lead from a mine." By 1720, maps identified it as "Riviere a la Mine" or "River of the Mine." By 1850, many lead mines existed in central and southern Missouri. Today, 92 percent of the U.S. primary lead supply comes from Missouri, making it the nation's leader and one of the top lead producers in the world.

93.0 Terraces

On the right, the farm fields have been terraced. Farmers make terraces in their fields to slow the runoff from rainfall or melting snow. They plow mounds or ridges of soil to curve along a slope making level areas to hold the moisture so it will soak into the soil for better crop production. When water runoff is slowed, less soil is carried away, preserving topsoil and reducing erosion. Farmers make parallel terraces of equal width so that an equal number of crop rows can be planted, thus making it easier to operate tractors, combines, and tillage tools. Long, gentle curves aid in making terraces farmable using commercial farm equipment. Just building the terrace does not assure erosion control. Farmers must regularly maintain terrace shape and restore ridge height. You will see more of this widespread and valuable farming practice over the next 5 miles, especially near mile markers 98 and 99.

95.0 Chouteau Creek

It seems fitting that this creek with this famous name is near the middle of the state. The Chouteau family had a huge role in settling Missouri from St. Louis to Kansas City. In 1764, Auguste Chouteau helped his stepfather, Pierre Laclede, set up a trading post and build St. Louis. In 1821, Auguste's nephew, François Chouteau, established a trading post at the confluence of the Kansas and Missouri rivers that began the growth of present-day Kansas City. Amazing that we so quickly cross over a tiny creek that honors such a grand family—the family that helped establish the two largest cities in Missouri.

96.0 Cooper County

You are in Cooper County, named after Benjamin Cooper. Cooper was born in Virginia, but he moved to Kentucky and then Missouri as the frontier boundaries moved west. He was a

The A. M. Scott *loading cargo at Arrow Rock landing, circa 1915 (Missouri Department of Natural Resources)*

colonel in the militia and was an associate of Daniel Boone during the Indian Wars. He first moved to this area with his wife and five sons in 1808. However, Governor Meriwether Lewis (of Lewis and Clark fame) ordered him to abandon his farm and return east because he was too far into Indian country and away from protection in the event of an Indian attack. He complied with Governor Lewis and relocated near the Loutre River (mile 169), but two years later he returned here with settlers from Kentucky, Tennessee, and Virginia.

97.0   Arrow Rock

Exit 98 takes you to Arrow Rock. Today only seventy-nine people live in Arrow Rock, but it was once a bustling town. Founded in 1829, Arrow Rock is where the steamship met the wagon—the intersection of the Santa Fe Trail and Missouri River. It became the largest river shipping town between St. Louis and Kansas City. By 1837, four warehouses along Arrow Rock's landing were supplying the southern United States with agricultural products and Missouri mules. But the railroad took the steam out of steamboat travel and the river channel gradually receded east. Arrow Rock saw its last ferry run in 1927. Arrow Rock is a National Historic Landmark and has been called the "most historic spot in Missouri." It is home to Missouri's first state historic site, quaint shops, restaurants, and the historic Lyceum Theatre. The name "Arrow Rock" came about because an outcropping of flint along the river made it an important manufacturing area for arrow points by Native Americans. You may have noticed the brown marker indicating that this stretch of I-70 is part of the Santa Fe Heritage Trail. For more information about the Santa Fe Trail see 107W (page 46).

98.0 Cooper County Fairgrounds

Ahead at mile 99.8 on the right (just past the overpass), you will see the Cooper County Fairgrounds. This fairground is unique in that the land is privately owned by a volunteer group and was purchased with funds donated from the community to "encourage youth to show their talents and grow in the agricultural community." When someone was awarded money for their "best of show," they often generously contributed their winnings back to the Fair Board. By the early 1960s, those funds enabled the Cooper County Agricultural and Mechanical Society to buy this land. Competitions reward youth who have worked hard grooming their animals and growing their crops. Besides competitions, county fairs entertain families with auctions, tractor pulls, greased-pig-chasing contests, carnival rides, and deep-fried fair food (the last two of which should never be mixed). A county fair brings rural communities together. It is a time for community members to socialize, foster community pride, and share and compare the fruits of their labors—products raised on their land or prepared in their kitchens. Gary Schmidt and Susan Felch, in their book, *Autumn: A Spiritual Biography of the Season*, capture the sensual nature of a trip to the county fair:

There is always the hawker barking out his hot dogs, always the rickety Tilt-a-Whirl run by a bored teenager, always the smell of cotton candy yielding to the smell of cow yielding to the smell of too many bodies too close yielding to the smell, the awful smell of pig. The crafts and quilts are always the same from year to year, as are the gigantic squash—and every year, we say the same thing: "How could it ever grow this big? And how would you ever lift the dang thing?"

100.0 From Rail to Trail

Just ahead the Katy Trail crosses above I-70 on an old railroad bridge. You will intersect this 225-mile-long hiking and biking trail two more times between here and St. Louis. The Katy Trail was built on the abandoned corridor of the Missouri-Kansas-Texas Railroad (called the MKT or Katy line). This trail is managed as a state park, and people can hop aboard the Katy Trail at twenty-six different trailheads or two fully restored depots. Many progressive states and towns have converted their abandoned railroad rights-of-way to recreational trails. The Katy Trail is the world's longest rail-to-trail conversion.

101.0 Boon or Boone?

Ahead is Boonville, named after the early explorer and settler Daniel Boone. You may have noticed that there is no "e" in this town named for the famous pioneer. Daniel's relatives were inconsistent in the spelling of their own name. Early maps of the area spelled it with and without the "e" too, probably following the inconsistent Boone family. Daniel's tombstone read "Boon" without the "e" and with the "N" carved backward.

102.0 Boone's Lick Country

This region is called Boone's Lick Country because the area's most famous salt lick was Boone's Lick (also spelled "Boon's Lick" or "Boonslick"). Daniel Boone's sons Nathan and Daniel Morgan Boone began making salt at a nearby lick originally called "Mackey's Lick." They would boil the salty water until it was sludge. Then it was dried and sent downriver to St. Louis. Salt was a critical and valuable resource because it was used for preserving food and tanning leather. A trail called the Boone's Lick Trail ran from St. Charles to Boone's Lick. Originally this trail was used by Indians, trappers, and fur traders. It is considered to be the grandfather of the Oregon and Santa Fe trails because travelers heading for those more famous trails used it to begin their journeys. The first stagecoach line traveled the trail in 1819 and soon Boone's Lick Trail became the most traveled road in Missouri. Boone's Lick Trail was the I-70 of the mid-1800s as immigrants, livestock, and supplies streamed west.

104.0 Interstate Ike

At the Rest Area you can read how in 1956 President Eisenhower began the world's largest public works project—the U.S. Interstate System. Eisenhower's experience traveling across the United States after World War I and then in Europe during World War II impressed upon him the need for efficient highways to move soldiers and equipment. Another goal of the Interstate Highway Act was to allow quick evacuations of all cities with a population of 50,000 or more in the event of an attack. The Interstate System was born out of a fear of nuclear war, not with family vacation travel in mind. Eisenhower apparently imagined the ultimate rush hour, but probably never envisioned daily rush hours that clog I-70 in Kansas City and St. Louis.

105.0 A "Fantastic Company"

Boonville has a colorful history. One Boonville tale is the story of the "Fantastic Company." From the time Missouri became a state and until 1847 a law required all male citizens between the ages of eighteen and forty-five to regularly meet and drill as a militia. Men who did not attend the militia muster would be fined a dollar for each day they missed. These musters became burdensome and were seen as a waste of time. In response to this unpopular law a group of Cooper County citizens secretly formed a militia company and called themselves the "Fantastic Company." They wore outlandish costumes and some carried broomsticks instead of guns. Some rode mules and donkeys instead of horses. All of this was to poke fun at the serious militias. One day while a state militia was formally mustered and ready to drill in front of the Boonville courthouse, the Fantastic Company approached and proceeded to drill. Colonel Turley, the leader of the state militia, upon seeing the mules and strange costumes and broomsticks recognized that this was an insult and ordered his men to surround the Fantastic Company. A fight ensued and flying stones and brickbats injured several men. One man was struck below his right eye and died two days later from this injury.

108.0 Nature's Sanitation Crew

When wildlife crosses I-70 they often don't make it. Yet an animal killed in nature does not go to waste. Something will eat it

Turkey vulture

and return it to the food chain. Such are the cycles of nature. If you are traveling during March through October, you may have already noticed the large black birds soaring above the countryside with upraised wings. If not, you have an excellent chance of seeing them flying above the Missouri River ahead. These amazing birds are turkey vultures—often called "buzzards." Vultures play an important ecological role in cleaning up and recycling dead animals, especially roadkills. Their bare red head resembles the head of a turkey, hence the name. The featherless head is an advantage. When sticking their heads into rotten roadkills imagine the matted mess of feathers that would result if they had feathers on their heads. Vultures have strong hooked beaks for tearing apart carcasses, but unlike hawks and eagles, vultures have weak feet because they do not need to kill their food. Watch these amazing flyers soar gracefully, rarely flapping their wings. Vultures need the updrafts or "thermals" to soar on, so don't expect to see flying vultures until midmorning when the sun heats up the ground and atmosphere. They can be easily identified in flight because, unlike eagles, they soar with their wings in a "V" with wing tips above the horizontal.

111.0 Floodplains, Flood Protection
Just before you cross the Missouri River (and Katy Trail again), you will cross the river's expansive floodplain, which includes

the Big Muddy National Wildlife Refuge, established in 1994. We often think of floods as being bad, but here floods are a great event. Floods create wetland habitats for wildlife and contribute rich nutrients to bottomland soils. Floodplains serve as enormous water storage areas in times of flooding. The low, flat area you pass over can become a lake during times of high water. Cutting the river off with levees from these natural storage areas increases flooding downstream. Allowing the river to leave its banks and expand into these plains reduces downstream flooding. Evidence of floodplain benefits is mounting in Missouri. The flood of 1993 forced more than 10,000 people from their homes and resulted in dozens of deaths and billions in property damage. After that flood, government agencies purchased more than 21,000 acres of floodplains in Missouri. Some levees were moved back away from the river and other areas were left open to future flooding. In 1995 and 2002, torrential rainstorms caused the National Weather Service to predict floods along the Missouri. But these floods never happened as the river had more room to spread out. Things generally turn out better when, instead of trying to corral Mother Nature, we let her "go with the flow."

113.0 "Too Thick to Drink, Too Thin to Plow"

That is how settlers described the muddy Missouri River. You will cross the Big Muddy ahead at mile 115. As you approach the bridge you cannot help but notice the spectacular white cliffs rising above the river. For centuries the river served as a highway and as a hunting and fishing resource for Native Americans and European settlers. Today this river is still a national treasure that serves mankind in many ways, including providing us with hydroelectric power, irrigation water, and transport for barges carrying asphalt, cement, sand, and grains such as wheat, soybeans, and corn. Jet skis, johnboats, and aluminum canoes ply the waters that had been navigated by dugout canoes of Native Americans and the steamships of settlers. The Mighty Mo' has also been a source of inspiration for poets and artists. When Walt Whitman experienced the river in 1865 he wrote,

Others may praise what they like;
But I, from the banks of the running Missouri, praise nothing
    in art,
Till it has well inhaled the atmosphere of this river, also the
    western prairie-scent,
And exudes it all again.

Even now as you cross the river you might get a sense of the atmosphere of the powerful and inspiring Missouri River.

115.0 Wine Country

Exit 115 leads to Rocheport, a river town filled with historic nineteenth-century buildings. On the way you will pass the Les Bourgeois Winery and the associated vineyards. Wine tasting and tours are available, along with a bistro with a bluff-top view of I-70 and the Missouri River. This is just one of Missouri's forty-seven wineries. The vineyards represent some of the 1,100 acres of grapes grown in Missouri. In 2003, more than 3.6 million bottles of Missouri wines were sold, bringing in $26 million in sales, $2 million in state tax revenue, and creating more than 250 jobs. A recent legislative proclamation named Norton/ Cynthiana the official grape of Missouri. Some vineyards can be seen briefly to the right just past the exit at the mile 116 sign.

116.0 Redcedars

The evergreen trees you see along the highway and scattered in the pastures are eastern redcedar. Redcedars are not really cedars; instead they are a member of the juniper family. They grow in open and sunny places. Because of its color, fragrance, and presumed ability to repel moths, redcedar wood is used for chests, wardrobes, and closet linings. Cedarwood oil is used for making many other fragrances. Woodenware and many wooden novelties sold at tourist attractions are made from redcedar. At one time most wooden pencils were made from redcedar and the tree was known as "pencil cedar," but now only about 10 percent of pencils are made from this tree. Redcedars are in the top five trees used for Christmas trees. Redcedars benefit wildlife as they provide year-round shelter from predators and the elements. Birds use them for nest sites and redcedar berries are eaten by many kinds of birds as well as raccoons, skunks, foxes, rabbits, and other mammals. A redcedar found on an undisturbed rocky bluff in Missouri has been estimated to be over 1,000 years old!

118.0 Corps of Discovery

Here you see one of the brown signs indicating the Lewis and Clark Trail. Their "trail" was the Missouri River and they traveled it across the state from the confluence of the Mississippi and Missouri through Kansas City in 1804. Thomas Jefferson sent Meriwether Lewis, William Clark, and their "Corps of Discovery" to explore the newly acquired Louisiana Purchase and search for a water route to the Pacific Ocean. Along the way they discovered animals, plants, and peoples. Their journals reveal details of these discoveries. For example, on June 6, 1804, very near the spot where you just crossed the Missouri, William Clark wrote that they saw "some buffalow Sign to day." This was their first mention of the 2,000-pound, 6-foot-tall creature that once roamed Missouri. You won't find such signs today. By the 1840s all of Missouri's buffalo (more accurately called "American Bison") had been killed for their hides and meat. Travel always involves discovery to those who take the time to notice things. Our hope is that you will be part of a "corps of discovery" as you drive across Missouri.

119.0 Boone County

Since crossing the Missouri River you have been in Boone County. This county was named for the famous trailblazer and wilderness scout, Daniel Boone, who claimed, "I have never been lost, but I will admit to being confused for several weeks." Although Boone is famous for his wilderness adventures in Kentucky, he moved to Missouri when he was 65 years old and some say that he spent the best years of his life here where he could hunt, trap, and explore new lands not yet crowded with people. In his twenty-one years in Missouri he saw the land change dramatically. When he first arrived in 1799 this land was ruled by Spain. Within a year of his arrival, France took ownership. Four years after his arrival, the United States claimed it in the Louisiana Purchase. When he died in 1820, his family buried him next

*Daniel Boone (Kansas City
Public Library, Missouri)*

to his wife in what is now Warren County. But in the 1840s a
cemetery company from Kentucky took the remains of Boone
and his wife back to Kentucky. The original tombstone is on
display at Central Methodist University in Fayette. The family
donated it with the stipulation that it never leaves the campus.
It is fitting that even after death he traveled through his beloved
forests on his way back to Kentucky.

Back at mile 98 you read about county fairs. The first county
fair west of the Mississippi was held in Boone County in 1835.

121.0 Pork Place

Ahead on the left just past the overpass is the headquarters of
the Missouri Pork Association where they support promotion,
research, education, and legislation all aimed at getting people
to "fork more pork." Missouri is seventh among states in pork
production, producing 6 percent of the nation's "other white
meat." This industry employs 25,000 Missourians and contributes more than $1 billion to the Missouri economy. Sometimes
pigs *do* fly—15 out of every 100 Missouri hogs are exported!

122.0 Perche Creek

For the last several miles you have been passing through some
beautiful rock cuttings along the highway. Long before our

highway cut through these rocks, streams and rivers coursed through them. Perche means "pierced" in French. Two hundred years ago this creek was named "Split Rock" or "roche perche." While this name accurately describes the steep limestone walls, just south of here, that rise up on either side of the creek and create a meandering furrow across the land, the most common story of how the creek got its name was from a "pierced rock" that was observed by William Clark on June 6, 1804. High on the wall of limestone a cave-like hole can still be seen today from the Katy Trail (see mile 100). Because of the radical shift of the Missouri River over time, this interesting rock, once at the original mouth of the creek, is now separated from the "Mighty Missouri" by a mile.

FROM COLUMBIA TO ST. LOUIS

123.0 Mizzou

Exit 128 takes you to the University of Missouri campus (MU), which was founded in 1839, making it the first public university west of the Mississippi River and the first state university in Thomas Jefferson's Louisiana Purchase territory. MU's tiger mascot was inspired by and named after a local Civil War militia called the Missouri Tigers. Today it is known as "Truman Tiger" in honor of Missouri's only U.S. president, Harry Truman. A distinctive feature of the campus is a row of six Ionic columns. These columns were part of the first building on campus, built between 1840 and 1843. This building burned to the ground in 1892 in a fire rumored to have been caused by the first electric lightbulb west of the Mississippi River. More than 5,000 trees and 650 varieties of plants accent the 1,358-acre campus with colorful flowers and, in the fall, brilliant leaves. The campus features eighteen buildings on the National Register of Historic Places, 600-year-old Chinese stone lions, and Thomas Jefferson's original tombstone. The student body is made up of more than 28,000 students from all fifty states and more than 100 countries. MU is widely known for its programs in journalism (the world's first journalism school was founded here in 1908), and such well-known current broadcast journalists as Jim Lehrer and Elizabeth Vargas graduated from here. Brad Pitt majored in journalism here with a focus on advertising. He left college two credits short of graduating to move to California. Other famous alumni include singer Sheryl Crow, actors George C. Scott and Tom Berenger, businessmen Edward D. Jones (founder of the investment firm) and Sam Walton (founder of Wal-Mart), and cartoonist Mort Walker, who created *Beetle Bailey*. A life-size statue of Beetle stands in front of the campus Alumni Center.

126.0 Hail Columbia

Several magazines and websites including *Money Magazine*, *Men's Journal*, and MSN.com have ranked Columbia as one of the best places to live. The name "Columbia" refers to Christopher Columbus and was the first popular name for our country. Many early leaders wanted the United States of America to be named "Columbia" because it was shorter and more poetic. Columbia became the female personification of America, similar to the male Uncle Sam. Today she is most often seen at the beginning of a movie made by Columbia Pictures. Nicknames for this city include "The Athens of Missouri" and "College Town USA" because it is home to three universities. Besides the University of Missouri, Stephens College and Columbia College are located in Columbia. Stephens College is a women's liberal arts college with particularly strong programs in fashion design, dance, and theater. Many Stephens students have gone on to excel on stage and screen, including such notables as Joan Crawford, Elizabeth Mitchell, Jennifer Tilly, Dawn Wells, and Paula Zahn. Columbia College also started out as a women's school, but it is now coed. Columbia College specializes in adult and military education. It serves nearly 25,000 college students each year at thirty-two campuses in eleven states, with fifteen campuses being located on military bases. As with most college towns, Columbia is known for its eclectic mix of restaurants, shops, art galleries, music venues, and coffeehouses.

128.0 Capital Highway

The next exit takes you south to Jefferson City, the capital of Missouri. Although I-70 misses this state capital by 30 miles, it passes through four other state capitals—the capitals of Colorado, Kansas, Indiana, and Ohio. Can you name them?

130.0 Hominy Creek

In 1896 this creek gained its culinary name from the settlers here who raised corn and made it into lye hominy. Hominy consists of dried corn kernels that have been soaked in lye so that the hulls are removed. Once the hard outer hull is removed the germ is easier to digest, more nutritious, and often considered tastier. As far back as 1500 to 1200 B.C., hominy was eaten in what is now Guatemala. Many Native Americans and the early colonists ate hominy. Hominy is boiled until cooked and served as either a cereal or vegetable. Hominy may also be pressed into patties and fried. Hominy ground into small grains is called "hominy grits." Hominy grits are a favorite food in the southern United States. In fact Georgia named it the "Official State Prepared Food." The Charleston *Post and Courier* said that a man full of grits is a man of peace.

132.0 Another Cat

Back at mile 27 you saw the yellow and black cat sign of Certified Scales. Ahead on the left at 133.0 you will see another yellow and black CAT sign indicating one of more than 200 Caterpillar dealerships in the United States. Caterpillar is the world leader in construction and mining equipment, manufacturing over 300 different machines. Their largest dump truck will not be seen on I-70. It is used only in mining. This truck is almost 24 feet high, 48 feet long (more than half a basketball court), and 30 feet wide, 6 feet wider than the two lanes of I-70 that you are driving on. CAT also makes engines for yachts and fishing boats and is the world's number one producer of electrical generators. Caterpillar was formed in 1925, but the two founders had been manufacturing steam and gas track-type tractors since the 1890s. The Allies used one of the first Caterpillar tractors in World War I. CAT equipment helped build I-70 and highways around the world. Now Caterpillar is working on projects that are out of this world as they collaborate with NASA to design construction equipment to be used to build a permanent base on the moon.

135.0 The Kingdom of Callaway

Ahead you will enter Callaway County, named for Captain James Callaway, grandson of Daniel Boone and veteran of the War of 1812. Callaway and three of his men were killed in an Indian ambush while crossing the Loutre River in 1815 in what is now neighboring Montgomery County. The bodies of the three soldiers were cut into many pieces and so were buried in a common grave, whereas Callaway's body was found several days later by a search party that included his father, who had come from St. Charles County to help look for it. Since the Civil War, this county has been referred to as the Kingdom of Callaway. Several accounts exist regarding how the county came to be known as a kingdom, but all accounts point to the fanatical Southern sympathies of the residents, some promoting the secession of Missouri from the Union. In 1861, Union troops advanced toward Fulton where all the young men were away at war. To protect their town from Yankee pillaging, the old men and boys used bravery and cunning. Armed with only their hunting rifles, they painted some logs black to look like cannons and lined them up for the Union to see. Union General John B. Henderson negotiated with Colonel Jefferson Franklin Jones and agreed not to invade Callaway if the colonel disbanded his men and their "artillery." This amounted to the county negotiating a treaty as a sovereign state with the U.S. government. Locals interpreted this treaty as recognizing their county's independence and right to govern itself as its own kingdom. The city ahead, called Kingdom City, reflects that you have entered the Kingdom of Callaway.

137.0 Little Dixie

The Little Dixie Wildlife Area (Exit 137) contains a fishing lake and trails, including a handicapped-accessible nature trail. This region is called "Little Dixie" because the residents were immigrants from Kentucky, Tennessee, Virginia, and the Carolinas. This area had the highest percentage of slaves in Missouri. Slaves mostly worked on farms. Since most farms were along the Missouri River because of the rich floodplain soils and because farm products could be shipped to market by boat, many slaves lived in these river counties you have been driving through. In 1860, Lafayette County had 6,374 slaves, whereas Boone had 5,034, Saline 4,876, and Callaway 4,523 slaves. Unlike the Deep South where large plantations held many slaves, these farms were small so Missouri farmers usually had only one or two slaves. During the Civil War many slaves fled their owners and set up their own self-reliant villages in this area still known as Little Dixie.

140.0 Growing Farm Fun

On the left is the big red barn of the Shryocks' Callaway Farm. This farm has been in operation since 1889. Today it is a family farm run by two brothers, their sons, and their families. They grow corn and soybeans on the 850-acre farm, but their fields also produce a healthy crop of fun. They offer hayrides, campfires, and amazing mazes cut into the cornfields. Many farmers are supplementing their traditional farm income by opening their farms to the public for agriculture-based recreation. This new industry is called "agritourism."

141.0 Soybeans

During summer, amid the cornfields, look for fields with rows of short bushy plants. After the leaves fall off you will see a two-foot-high plant with bean pods hanging from it. You use soybean products every day. Hundreds of food products use protein-rich soymilk or flour. Other products such as candles, crayons, ink, body lotions, shampoos, hair conditioners, paint removers, fabric conditioners, and biodiesel fuel are all made from soybeans. Missouri is "home to soy biodiesel," as the University of Missouri did the original testing. Other states provide energy from oil fields, but Missouri provides clean-burning fuel from its soybean fields. The Chinese discovered this plant 2,000 years ago and by 220 A.D. they were making soymilk and tofu.

142.0 Advertising Barns

The old barn on the left (mile 143) is being used as an advertisement for Meramec Caverns. In the early 1930s, the owner of Meramec Caverns took a trip to Florida looking for work and noticed signs painted on barns encouraging travelers to "See Rock City" or "Chew Mail Pouch Tobacco." He decided to use barn painting for his caverns. During the heyday of barn advertisements in the 1950s, more than 300 barns in twenty-six states from Michigan to California had signs for Meramec Caverns. Originally, in return for allowing the Meramec Caverns sign to be painted on their barn, the barn owner was given a railroad pocket watch, the wife was given a box of chocolates, and the whole family was given a free pass into Meramec Cave. But the biggest incentive was that the entire barn would receive a fresh coat of paint. As barns disappear such ads are becoming scarce. Zoning laws prevent new ads from being painted. Only eighty-two Meramec barns in five states remain. Dedicated hobbyists travel all over the United States searching for and photographing the few remaining advertising barns. An early owner of Meramec Caverns also is credited with inventing the bumper sticker. Cardboard "bumper signs" were tied onto people's bumpers with twine. Early versions had wax paper backing that would be peeled off to expose flypaper-like glue. Politicians made bumper stickers commonplace in the 1960s but created bad feelings about them by using glue that made it difficult to remove the stickers.

144.0 Tucker Prairie

One mile ahead on the right is the Tucker Prairie Natural Area. This 146-acre prairie is owned by the University of Missouri and is used for class projects and research on such topics as the effects of haying and burning on grassland plants. The word "prairie" comes from the French word for a grassy meadow. Prairies are a mix of grasses and wildflowers and so you may notice flowers mixed with native grasses such as little bluestem and Indian grass. These hardy plants have extensive root systems that tap into groundwater up to 15 feet below the surface. This ensures their survival even in the hottest Missouri summers. When Europeans first traveled to Missouri, prairie grasses and wildflowers blanketed 15 million acres (one-third of the state). Today because of conversion to croplands and urban uses, only 90,000 acres of this original prairie remain. But these remaining prairies are amazingly diverse. Over 800 plant species occur in Missouri prairies; 224 different kinds of plants have been found on Tucker Prairie alone.

146.0 Winston Churchill Memorial

If you take Exit 148 south to Fulton, you can visit the Winston Churchill Memorial where he made his famous "Iron Curtain" speech in 1946. With help from President Harry Truman, the president of Westminster College, Franc L. McCluer, scheduled Churchill to speak at the school. Before his speech he dined on country ham and fried chicken at the home of McCluer and eloquently declared, "The pig has reached its highest point of evolution in this ham." On March 5, 1946, a crowd estimated at 25,000 people came out to hear his speech, "The Sinews of Peace." National media descended upon the town and the speech was broadcast live on each of the four national radio networks. As Churchill spoke of the threat of Soviet Communism in post–World War II Europe he told the crowd, "From Stettin in the Baltic to Trieste in the Adriatic, an iron curtain has descended across the continent." Even though, at the time, most people doubted such a growth of Soviet Communism, Churchill had accurately predicted, from the little town of Fulton, Missouri, changes that would affect the whole world.

147.0 Firefighters Memorial

At the Mid Missouri Tourism Center ahead (Exit 148), there is a memorial dedicated to Missouri firefighters. To your left from I-70 you can see this larger-than-life sculpture of a firefighter with head in hand and on bended knee. If you visit the site you can step along bricks that pave the "Walk of Honor" and that lead to a memorial wall that lists the names of firefighters who have died in the line of duty. Fred Turnbull, of the St. Louis Volunteer Fire Department, begins this list that extends from 1838 through the present decade. A 2-by-3-foot piece of the New York World Trade Center is also displayed to honor firefighters.

150.0 The Missouri Farm

The Missouri Farm on your right is not your typical family farm. Instead it is a private research farm where scientists conduct studies to improve agricultural production. You may have noticed the silver structures at many farms along I-70. These are grain storage bins. Here at the Missouri Farm you see what are nicknamed "spiderweb" bins because of the central tower with multiple chutes radiating out and down from it. After harvest,

Missouri firefighter

grain is elevated from trucks by a conveyor in the central tower. The grain is then directed into the appropriate chute and down into the round bin. You'll see another cluster of storage bins at mile 160 ahead.

151.0 **Callaway Livestock Center**

Ahead on the right is the Callaway Livestock Center where John Payne Harrison and his son sell more than 124,000 head of cattle each year. John grew up in the cattle sales business. It is the only life he has ever known and he never thought about doing anything else. The first livestock sale in Callaway County was held on February 1, 1876, and a weekly livestock sale has been held here ever since. In 1876, the sales commission earned by the auctioneer was 2.5 percent. It has never changed and is still 2.5 percent today. The Callaway Livestock Center has been in the Harrison family since 1904. In the early days mules were sold and then driven to Mississippi by a fourteen-year-old boy. The mules would follow the boy and a white horse with a cowbell around its neck. John still has the cowbell that led the mules to Mississippi. Today most livestock comes from within a 100-mile radius, but some cattle come from as far away as Illinois and

Nebraska to be sold. Cattle bought here are shipped all over the United States.

152.0 "Wood" You Believe What Comes from Wood?

As you pass through this forest you'll see different kinds of trees such as oak, cottonwood, sycamore, and walnut. Besides the many wood products mentioned back at mile 82, more than 5,000 other products are made from the fibers and chemicals in wood. "Woody" products that may be traveling with you today include the gum you're chewing and the paper it's wrapped in; the crayons and coloring book the kids are using in the backseat; your suitcase; the toothpaste, cosmetics, prescription drugs, soap, shoes, and shoe polish in your suitcase; sandwich bags and the dried fruit inside them; your ice cream snack, tea, or coffee; disposable diapers, the car upholstery, the rubber in your tires, your vehicle's paint, and the steering wheel that guides you!

153.0 River of Mud

Lucky for you, a nicely paved bridge passes over the Auxvasse Creek as you travel I-70. Before such concrete conveniences, a group of Frenchmen traveled through this area with Lilburn Boggs, who later became a governor of Missouri. Upon crossing the river, they became stuck in the mud and so aptly named the waterway the "Riviere aux Vases," which translates to "River of Mud."

154.0 Yellow Signs

Along the highway fence line you may have noticed tent-shaped yellow signs with black numbers on them such as the one back at 153.8 and ahead at 158.2 and 160.3. Utility companies use these signs to mark underground natural gas or oil pipelines or other corridors. The signs are angled so that the numbers are markers for airplanes searching for leaks, vegetation that needs to be removed, unauthorized construction, or other encroachments in the corridor. The orange signs along the fence mark the fiber-optic communication cables mentioned back at 51. These colors, along with blue for water, are the commonly used colors to indicate the type of buried utility.

155.0 "Where Caring Counts"

This is the motto of Missouri Girls Town, seen on the left (155.6), a residential treatment facility for girls, ages eight to twenty-one, who have been abused or neglected. The mission is to create a loving, stable environment for the girls' care and treatment and help them develop the life skills they will need as adults. The General Federation of Missouri Women's Clubs founded Missouri Girls Town in 1953. Each year Girls Town provides care for nearly 100 girls from across the state of Missouri. That a town named "Bachelor" (because when founded it had a high population of single men) is near this place called "Girls Town" is mere serendipity.

159.0 Slowing Water

Over the next two miles you can see grass waterways, strips of grass in low drainage areas of cropland. Like the terraces mentioned back at mile 93, the grass slows the rainwater running off the fields. Because rainwater moves soil particles into streams and rivers that ultimately flow to the sea, and because soil is made of tiny particles worn from rocks, people say soil is "rocks on their way to the sea." This washing away of soil particles is called erosion. A field covered in grass erodes at a rate 4,000 times less than a bare field. Unfortunately Missouri ranks third in the nation in soil loss due to erosion. One hundred million tons of soil erodes in Missouri annually. That's enough soil to cover all four lanes of I-70 from Kansas City to St. Louis 35 feet deep! You will see more grass waterways at miles 171 and 172 and other locations ahead. By preventing soil from moving toward the sea, farmers keep cropland productive and Missouri's streams clean. They take the long-term view that "we do not inherit the land from our fathers, we borrow it from our children."

158.0 Power to the People

Follow the high-voltage power line to the southern horizon to find the hourglass-shaped cooling tower of Ameren's Callaway Nuclear Power Plant. Over the next 10 miles you can glimpse the 553-foot-tall cooling tower. On cold winter days a plume of steam will make it easier to locate. Power plants, whether coal-fired or

Ameren Callaway Nuclear Power Plant

nuclear, heat water to make steam to turn turbines that create electricity. Water from the Missouri River is pumped 5 miles to the plant through a 48-inch-diameter underground pipe. After being heated to create the steam, the water goes to the cooling tower. The tower can cool 585,000 gallons per minute from 125 degrees to 95 degrees. About 15,000 gallons per minute are lost out the top through evaporation and another 5,000 gallons per minute are sent back to the Missouri River. The Callaway Nuclear Power Plant creates enough electricity each year to meet the energy needs of more than 840,000 households.

160.0 Farm Pond Fun

Farm ponds such as the one you see here provide drinking water for livestock and store water runoff, thereby reducing soil erosion. But ponds offer many recreation benefits as well. They offer excellent fishing opportunities, and not just for children, but for serious anglers. Seven of Missouri's record fish came from farm ponds, including the biggest white crappie, black crappie, and bluegill. Missouri leads the nation with more than 300,000 private ponds and lakes. The Missouri Department of Conservation (MDC) will stock private ponds at no cost as long as they meet certain criteria, such as being at least 8 feet deep.

The MDC stocks about 650 ponds (1,000 acres of water) annually. Typical stocking rates are 100 bass, 500 bluegill, and 100 catfish for every surface acre of water. Within two or three years these ponds produce keeper-sized fish and lots of fun.

161.0 Hedgerows

On the right is a hedgerow, a strip of trees bordering fields. Many hedgerows have short, rounded trees called Osage-orange or "hedge." Before barbed wire fences, hedgerows were planted to serve as natural fences. Osage-orange is a dense, bushy tree with thorns on the branches. When planted close together they make an impenetrable fence touted as being "horse-high, bull-strong, and pig-tight." Osage-orange wood is so strong that it was used to make wagon wheels. Now it is used to make fence posts, crossties, and archery bows. The hedge apple is a nonedible, softball-sized yellow-green fruit that is lumpy and contains a sticky milky juice. Some people put hedge apples in their homes to repel spiders and insect pests.

165.0 Montgomery County

You've just entered Montgomery County. Like many Missouri counties, this county is named after a Revolutionary War hero. Richard Montgomery was born in Ireland and served as a captain in the British army before settling in New York. He became a courageous officer in the Continental army and led troops that captured Montreal from the British, but later was killed attempting to conquer the city of Quebec.

166.0 Oaks, Hickories, and You

Oak and hickory trees dominate in the state. In fact nearly three-quarters of Missouri's timberland is the oak-hickory type of forest. Twenty-one different kinds of oak and eight species of hickory grow in Missouri forests. Hickory is a strong wood that is used for striking-tool handles like hatchets, axes, and hammers. If you want to see a sampling of this forest up close, take the exit for the rest stop. Here you can see some red oak trees and sit at picnic tables in the shade of a grove of shagbark hickory—the most common hickory north of the Missouri River. By looking at their shaggy bark, you'll see where they get their name.

Sitting on Slave Rock (Montgomery County Historical Society)

167.0 Loutre River

In French *loutre* means "otter." Early French trappers must have encountered the river otter in this river they named "Loutre." Today you can encounter otters in every county in Missouri. Read more about Missouri otters at 168W (page 28).

168.0 Slave Rock

The sandstone rock formation on the grass slope in the center median has been the site of extremes in human emotions and activity. Some local historians believe it was used for slave auctions prior to the Civil War, although firm evidence is lacking. In the 1890s and early 1900s the Graham family, who owned the land, and their friends had Sunday afternoon picnics on the rock. Decades later it was a popular rest stop for weary travelers on old Highway 40. When the interstate was being built, a local woman fought successfully to have the interstate split to avoid destroying this historic rock that has witnessed such sadness and joy.

169.0 The Cave State

Missouri has been called the "Cave State" because it is home to 6,200 caves. At Exit 170 you can visit one of these caves at Graham Cave State Park, a National Historic Landmark on the

Danville Female Academy Complex (Montgomery County Historical Society)

banks of the Loutre River. For a story about a cave dweller see 172W (page 27).

170.0 Protected by Petticoats

On the left at 170.8 the white building in the trees is a Civil War–era structure that tells an exciting tale. The large white building just between the trees was once the chapel of the Danville Female Academy from 1853 to 1865. On October 14, 1864, Confederate troops, led by "Bloody" Bill Anderson, arrived in town. Looking for Union troops, they demanded the keys to the girls' school. To protect their school, some of the clever ladies claimed that they were Southern girls. There are a few versions of how the girls' petticoats "saved the school." One tale claims that a girl hung her petticoat over the school door as a sign of truce, whereas a children's book about the incident says that the girls waved them out the windows in support of the troops. Either way, the school was saved by the brave and clever women—and at least one white petticoat.

171.0 Power Lines

Electricity travels great distances before reaching our homes. The power lines crossing the highway ahead bring power from the Callaway Nuclear Power Plant (mile 158) to a substation at Montgomery City north of I-70. From there it enters a grid that serves 1.2 million customers all over central and eastern Missouri from the Bootheel to the Iowa border in the north. Power lines are constructed to carry different amounts of electricity. Voltage is the pressure that moves current through the lines. To move electricity through your home takes 115 volts. About 6,900 volts are used to move power through lines along city streets or out to farms. To send power across Missouri requires much bigger lines. The electric line here carries 345,000 volts because it is more efficient to send electricity cross-country at high voltages. You can tell the line carries high voltage because the cables are spaced far apart and long insulators are used to attach the cables to the tower frames. Those insulators are a string of ceramic bells hooked together to assure that the high voltage will not cause the current to jump across. In your home wiring, this is accomplished with a layer of insulating tape. As the voltage increases, it requires a greater and greater separation. So when you see an electric line, notice how long the insulators suspending the cables are; the longer they are, the higher the voltage. Along with longer, heavier insulators it takes bigger cables to carry more power. This heavier construction demands more rugged towers to support the lines.

174.0 Hermann

Hermann is a historic town on the banks of the Missouri River, 13 miles south of I-70. Wine making is not a new, trendy activity in Hermann. In 1837, German settlers founded Hermann, which eventually became home to sixty wineries. In 1848, Hermann held its first grape harvest festival and by 1856, Hermann was producing over 500,000 bottles of wine per year! Vines from Missouri were sent to both French and Californian vineyards, in the 1870s and 1890s respectively, to help rebuild their pest-infected vineyards. In the 1880s, Missouri was second only to New York in U.S. wine production. Today Hermann is home to four wineries and its German heritage is displayed and celebrated at the Deutschheim Historic Site, where visitors can see nineteenth-century German Americana artifacts, including grapevines planted 150 years ago.

176.0 Tree Farm

Thomas Fuller said, "He that plants a tree loves others besides himself." On the right is Hoette Farms & Nursery, a 420-acre wholesale nursery with over 180,000 ornamental, shade, and evergreen trees of varying sizes ready to be planted. The trees in this nursery, like other crops, are bred to resist disease or drought and to speed up growth rates. To harvest this crop, trees are machine-dug with large tree spades and placed in wire baskets with trunk protectors before being transported to the customer. The planting of a tree is a demonstration of hope and a gift of beauty to the next generation.

178.0 Missouri Manufacturing

Ahead on the right is the DuroFlex factory and on the left is the Christy Minerals factory. DuroFlex manufactures corrugated and fiberboard cartons, plastic shipping containers, plywood and fiberboard packaging components, and packaging for hazardous waste. Christy Minerals mines and processes clays for brick, tile, cement, floor tile, and ceramic industries. Many of their products are resistant to high temperatures, having such uses as lining furnace walls, but Christy also specializes in high-quality clay used by potters and other artisans. Both of these companies ship their products all over the United States, so you may have a piece of pottery in your home made from Christy clay that came shipped in a box from DuroFlex.

179.0 Manufacturing Happiness

Ahead one mile you will see a huge bull and a 40-foot Ferris wheel on the left. This is Tinsley's Amusements, which provides carnival rides, food stands, and games for state fairs, county fairs, carnivals, and neighborhood, school, or church festivals throughout Illinois and Missouri. Rich Tinsley has been in the amusement business since 1946 when as a nine-year-old he helped his dad rent and run two peddle-car kiddie rides. Since beginning his own show in 1971, Tinsley's amusement business has grown to be the largest in Missouri with more than eighty rides. He also places carousels and merry-go-rounds in shopping malls. The bull came from a friend in Kentucky and since the 1980s it has been "part of the family." The Ferris wheel (lit in festive lights at night) has been well traveled. Tinsley bought the Ferris wheel in 1954 and placed it at Holiday Hill Amusement Park in St. Louis. During each winter it was moved down to Miami and placed on top of buildings as a Christmas decoration. After this park closed it was moved to the Coney Island boardwalk, then to the Poconos, and then back to St. Louis's

Tinsley's bull and Ferris wheel

Union Station until 1998. You might also glimpse a small train and track that had been at the St. Louis Zoo. Tinsley and his small staff do everything from driving the trucks, preparing and laying out the site, setting up and tearing down rides, to operating the ride or game. In spite of the hard work, Tinsley loves his lifelong mission of manufacturing happiness for thousands of people each season.

181.0 Grass Farm

You may never have thought of lawn grass as being a crop, but at the Florissant Sod Farm on the left, it is their only crop. With more than 300 acres it is one of the largest sod farms in Missouri. Owner Richard Meyer faces the same challenges of any other farmer with concerns about weather, diseases, fertilizers, topsoil, experimenting with new varieties, planting, harvesting, and moving the "crop" to market. He grows zoysia, fescues, and bluegrasses on his irrigated fields. About 150 acres per year are harvested using a high-tech sod harvester pulled behind a tractor. This precision harvester controls the depth of the cut (taking a half inch of topsoil) and the length of the 42-inch-wide strips. As it cuts the sod, it rolls the strips into one-ton "balls." It can also cut 20-by-40-inch mats of sod. Harvest can take place anytime the ground is not too wet or frozen. The sod is sent to commercial and residential developments and athletic fields.

182.0 Roadside Advertising

You have, without a doubt, read at least one billboard as you have traveled across I-70 today and maybe even used one to direct you somewhere. You are one of about 42,000 people to-day who will view the billboard you see ahead at Exit 183. These outdoor advertisements have been a point of controversy in Missouri. While billboards help travelers find services and help retailers and landowners gain revenue, others find them an eye-sore on the landscape where they are believed to have become so abundant that it is difficult to see beyond the billboards. Ac-cording to the group "Save Our Scenery," Missouri has 14,000 billboards—about three times as many per mile as eight neigh-boring states. It could be worse. The Missouri Department of Transportation guidelines state that it is possible to have a bill-board placed every 1,400 feet on the same side of the highway, which would allow a maximum of 950 billboards along the east-bound side of I-70 across Missouri and another 950 along the westbound side! In 2006, advertisers in the United States spent $6.8 billion on outdoor advertising and pay between $300 to $2,000 a month to promote their products along the roadways. Roadside advertising is nothing new. In 1872, the International Billboard Poster's Association of North America began right here in Missouri.

185.0 Why Are Most Barns Red?

Ahead on the left at 185.4 is a red barn. We often think of barns as being red. Why red? Some believe that farmers merely chose that color to provide sharp contrast with the green landscape. But a more accurate explanation may be that for many years the ingredients for red paint were cheap and easy to mix. Iron ox-ide powder would give a deep red color. Mixed in linseed oil, it could be spread on the barn boards. When a little casein (as in white glue) was added, the protective coating had a longer life. Casein adhesive comes from skimmed milk, which was always available on the farm. So for generations red barns were most common. With today's ready-to-use paint, white and other col-ors have become popular for painting barns.

186.0 Common County

You are now in Warren County. Warren is a common county name. At least thirteen eastern and midwestern states have a county named Warren, honoring General Joseph Warren, a

Revolutionary War soldier who died at the Battle of Bunker Hill in Boston.

187.0 Meadowlane Farms

Meadowlane Farms on the hill to the left now grows wheat, corn, and soybeans on 85 acres of cropland. As you might guess by the white fence, it used to be a horse farm. The unusual tall tower at 187.8 was used to observe and photograph the quarter horses working out on a track.

188.0 Lifelines

In urban areas, concrete dividers separate the eastbound and westbound lanes of I-70. But here in the country, steel cables divide lanes whenever the median is between 36 and 60 feet wide and traffic exceeds 20,000 vehicles per day. Missouri is one of at least twenty-five states to invest in cables designed to block vehicles from crossing over the median into oncoming traffic. Although they cost $110,000 per mile to install and $12,000 per mile annually to maintain, these barriers have improved the safety of I-70. Crossover fatalities along Missouri interstate highways dropped from fifty-five, the year before cables were installed, to two in 2007. Critics of these cables state that they can cause high-centered vehicles to flip upon impact, cause additional damage to cars involved in minor accidents, and prevent emergency vehicles from making U-turns to administer help. But overall, transportation safety professionals are convinced that these lifelines save lives.

192.0 Elbow Room

Warrenton is the county seat of Warren County. Daniel Boone's daughter and son-in-law Flanders Callaway built a home south of here near the Missouri River. Daniel Boone was said to have "found elbow room" in what is now Warren County and was buried here in 1820. In the mid-1820s Daniel's son, Nathan, befriended a neighbor, Gottfried Duden, who influenced thousands of people to move to Missouri and fill up the countryside. Duden moved from Germany to Warren County in 1824 with the hopes of finding a place where his fellow countrymen could escape from the social, economic, and political problems in Germany. In 1829, he published a report of his journey. He praised

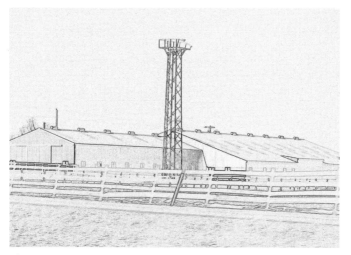

Observation tower

U.S. democracy and the affordable land that could be found in Missouri. German emigrants, inspired by his report, settled in Warren County and eventually throughout the state. Today the county's 30,000 residents are finding even less elbow room as the St. Louis metropolitan area encroaches into the county.

198.0 Repeater Station

The brick bank building on the left (198.8) was built in 1930 as a Bell System telephone repeater station. Repeater stations, now made obsolete by communication satellites, were the storehouses for equipment that strengthened the audio waves in long-distance phone calls, keeping conversations with friends and family audible and free of static interference. This repeater station was the first of three that were built between St. Louis and Kansas City. You may recall seeing another one back at mile 51.

199.0 Wright City

In 1857, Doctor Henry C. Wright platted this village along the new North Missouri Railroad, which had just been constructed. In 1863, Union soldiers raided Wright City and burned down the Baptist church, blacksmith shop, and Kennedy's Saloon—all known to be places where Southern sympathizers congregated.

Wright City businesses benefited first by being along the railroad, then by being along Highway 40, which ran through the center of town, and now they benefit from being along I-70.

200.0 Commerce and Congestion

As you approach St. Louis you will be surrounded by chaotic congestion bred by commerce. Its central location and confluence of two of the world's longest rivers make this part of Missouri a beehive of commercial activity. You will share the highway with more than 75,000 other vehicles that use this highway each day. St. Louis has the ninth-worst commute congestion in America. And the congestion is not just on the highways. St. Louis is ranked as the number two inland port in the United States for commercial cargo. This congestion and commerce is not new. Between 1850 and 1870 steamboats would be anchored three deep and for a mile along the levee in St. Louis. On land, trails and rails led from these rivers moving people and products west. Settlers streamed along the Boone's Lick Trail (102E) that closely paralleled the route of I-70 and led to the jumping-off points of the Oregon and Santa Fe trails. The railroad on the right, originally called the North Missouri Railroad and then the Wabash and now the Norfolk and Southern, replaced the wagons, coaches, and horse and oxen traffic of trails. In the first half of the twentieth century the automobile and U.S. 40 (53E), seen again here on the right, replaced much of the rail passenger travel. The original U.S. 40, in turn, was replaced by Interstate 70. If you get stopped in I-70 traffic jams it might make you feel better to remember that with your heat/AC, radio, CD/DVD players, smooth pavements, and quiet cars, you are traveling more comfortably and efficiently than those who traveled toward St. Louis in the past. And the silver lining of being surrounded by semi-trucks is that no matter how bad the economic news on your car radio, each truck loaded with goods is a sign of positive economic activity.

203.0 Foristell

Foristell is another railroad town. Settlement here began when the railroad was built in 1856. The community grew during the Civil War when a mill and a tobacco factory were established.

The town is named after Pierre Foristell, a respected wealthy local farmer and cattle rancher.

204.0 St. Charles County

You are now in St. Charles County. Two famous frontiersmen settled in this county. Daniel and Rebecca Boone settled about 20 miles south of here in 1799, and Jean Baptiste Pointe du Sable, a fur trader of African descent who is often considered to be the founder of Chicago, moved here a few years after Boone. It was originally organized by William Clark (of Lewis and Clark fame) as a district that extended north to Canada and west to the Pacific Ocean. Although the boundaries have shrunk, the county's population continues to grow.

205.0 Railroads

On the right you see the Norfolk and Southern tracks. The construction of railroads in Missouri started on a large scale in 1851, and until the 1920s, when autos and paved highways finally crossed the country, every facet of life was affected by the railroad. Railroads determined land values and locations of towns. Railroads moved people and products across Missouri, and they still do. Missouri has 4,400 miles of main track, 2,500 miles of yard track, and about 7,000 crossings. A total of nineteen railroads operate in the state: four large national railroads; two regionals, which only operate in two or three states; two terminal railroads, which are based in metropolitan areas; six short lines, regional railroads inside state lines; three tourist trains that haul passengers for short excursions; and Amtrak, the national passenger system. Amtrak offers daily trains between Kansas City and St. Louis.

206.0 Crossroads of the Nation

Wentzville calls itself "Crossroads of the Nation" because it is at the junction of I-70 and U.S. Highways 40 and 61, which becomes I-64. Between 2000 and 2004 the population of Wentzville grew by 41 percent making it the second fastest-growing city in Missouri. The George Thorogood song "Going Back to Wentzville" honors the fact that Wentzville is home to the legendary R&B and rock and roll icon Chuck Berry. Wentzville was founded in 1855 as a depot on the Northern Missouri Railroad. It was named after Erasmus Livingston Wentz, a railroad engineer for the line.

210.0 Ameren Sioux Power Plant

The striped smokestack on the horizon to the left is the Ameren Sioux Power Plant. Back at mile 158 you saw Ameren's nuclear-powered plant. This coal-fired power plant was the first in Missouri to burn chipped rubber tires to augment coal as a fuel source to create the steam to turn the turbines that make electricity. This plant burns more than 20,000 tons of tire chips annually—the equivalent of 25,000 tons of coal per year—providing electricity for more than 4,000 residential customers. This consumes more than 2.5 million discarded tires each year. The tires on your car might end up here someday and help meet Missouri's energy needs.

211.0 Van Plant

The large brown building on the left horizon beyond the trees is a GM assembly plant. Depending on the season, you may need to look back over your shoulder at 211.8 to see the assembly center. This is a 3.7 million-square-foot facility (77 acres under one roof). It is the only factory that produces the full-size Chevrolet Express and GMC Savana vans. In recent years, this plant has been the most productive large van plant in North America, investing 24.4 hours of labor per vehicle, resulting in forty-two vehicles produced per hour over two shifts.

212.0 Planned City

To your right you can glimpse Lake St. Louis. Lake St. Louis is not only a lake but also a city. In the 1960s, its founder R. T. Crow had visited two "new towns," Reston, Virginia, and Columbia, Maryland. Unlike most towns that grow from small settlements in an unplanned way, new towns are complete communities designed and built around detailed master plans on previously undeveloped land. Crow was convinced that this area was an excellent location for a first-class new town. Construction on the dam to create the lake began in 1968, and Lake St. Louis became a city in 1975. As was anticipated by its developers, it is one of the fastest-growing towns in Missouri. Three-

Ameren Sioux Power Plant

time Grammy-winning rap and hip-hop singer and actor Nelly has a home on Lake St. Louis.

215.0 Limestone Quarry

On the left is one of eleven quarries owned by Fred Weber, Inc. More than 1.5 million tons of stone have been removed from this quarry in a single year. Various stone construction aggregates are mined and shipped from here, including gravel for roads, driveways, and building sites, as well as material for making asphalt.

216.0 O'Fallon

This city was named for Maj. John O'Fallon, who was the nephew of explorer William Clark of Lewis and Clark fame. John O'Fallon became rich by buying and selling supplies to the army. He invested his newly acquired wealth in railroads. He was one of the promoters of the Pacific Railroad (later Missouri Pacific) as well as the North Missouri Railroad (later the Wabash) and the Ohio and Mississippi (later Baltimore and Ohio) and was the first president of each of these railroads. Today most people would probably think of a railroad alongside their property as a noisy nuisance, but back in the mid-1800s people fought to have them come through their land. Railroads were essential for commerce and growth. Before highways, towns that were not on railroads or rivers seldom survived. German immigrant Judge Arnold Krekel, of the U.S. District Court, welcomed the railroad through his property in 1854 and named the area for his friend O'Fallon in 1856. Because of its importance, during the Civil War the locals protected the railroad. German immigrants formed a Union regiment to defend the North Missouri Railroad line because railroads were a popular target for the Confederacy. Krekel led the regiment, called "Krekel's Dutch." Between 1990 and 2007, O'Fallon grew from 17,000 to 74,000 residents. It is now the eighth-largest city in the state. O'Fallon is headquarters for MasterCard's Global Technology and Operations Center.

218.0 T. R. Hughes Field

The next exit takes you to T. R. Hughes Field, home of the River City Rascals baseball team. The Rascals play professionally in the Frontier League. The 5,000-seat stadium combines old traditions and new amenities. With a nod toward the past, it features a St. Charles County Sports Hall of Fame, a manual scoreboard, and the players enter the field from centerfield as in the old days. New amenities include a hot tub party deck and a playground with swings, slides, and even basketball courts.

220.0 St. Peters

French trappers and traders settled here in the eighteenth century. German Catholics joined them in the early 1800s. The town of St. Peters (Exit 222) was named after the first church in the area, a 35-by-25-foot log church built in 1815 called "St. Peters on Dardenne Creek." By the late 1800s, the town had two railroad depots, hotels, saloons, and bustling shops. You can see the steeple of the Gothic All Saints Church on the right. The log church on Dardenne Creek was replaced because the creek frequently flooded making it difficult for parishioners to get to church. This church was built in 1874.

224.0 Magellan Oil Tanks

The white tanks to your right are part of a petroleum terminal owned by Magellan Midstream Partners. At this site seven tanks

All Saints Church

store 212,600 barrels of premium and regular unleaded gas and diesel. Magellan has twenty-seven such terminals, including seven marine terminals that store and distribute petroleum products such as gasoline, diesel, crude, and jet fuel. Magellan also has an 8,500-mile petroleum pipeline that distributes refined petroleum products to thirteen midwestern states and an 1,100-mile ammonia pipeline that delivers ammonia from production facilities in Texas and Oklahoma throughout the Midwest for use as agricultural fertilizer. You may have noticed the small trailers with white tanks of ammonia being pulled behind farm tractors or parked on farmsteads.

The large (12-foot-diameter) white ball on the tower to the right at 224.6 housed a weather radar. Read about this radar site and modern weather radars at 226W (page 13).

225.0 Nation's First Interstate

When the Federal-Aid Highway Act was signed in 1956, the Missouri State Highway Department was ready to spring into action and build its portion of the interstate system. The department had already made plans to improve portions of U.S. Highway 40 by upgrading it to a four-lane, controlled-access highway, so it was easy to relabel this project and include it in the new interstate program. Thus, on August 2, 1956, the Missouri State

Highway Commission approved construction of this portion of Interstate 70 in St. Charles County. Within a few weeks of these contracts being let, a concrete roadway was poured along I-70 in St. Charles making this stretch the first interstate highway.

226.0 St. Charles

In 1804 William Clark and his Corps of Discovery camped here for six days as they reloaded their supplies upon their keelboat and one of their pirogues, finished hiring the last of their crew members, and awaited the arrival of the other famous captain of the journey—Captain Meriwether Lewis. With the entire crew now assembled, they set off from here on their historic journey up the Missouri River to the Pacific Ocean. Thousands of travelers followed, as St. Charles became the eastern end of stagecoach lines and a jumping-off point for supply shipments and travelers heading west to Kansas City. St. Charles was Missouri's first capital. While the permanent capitol was being built in centrally located Jefferson City, legislators needed a place to conduct governmental affairs. Several cities vied for the honor of hosting the temporary seat of government. St. Charles was chosen after its citizens pledged free meeting space. On June 4, 1821, elected delegates met for the first time on the second floors of two adjoining buildings. These buildings provided space for the Senate and House and smaller quarters for the governor's office and a meeting room. Heated debates about state's rights and slavery filled these rooms until October 1, 1826, when the building in Jefferson City was completed. To visit the first capitol, take Exit 228.

228.0 Mighty, Modified, Muddy Missouri

Ahead you'll once again cross the Missouri River. It has been 115 road miles and 155 river miles since you last crossed it west of Columbia. It is now only 30 miles from where it flows into the Mississippi, nearly doubling the volume of water in that river. From its headwaters in Montana, to the confluence with the Mississippi just ahead, the Missouri River will have traveled 2,341 miles and dropped 3,600 feet in elevation. Here you will see that the river has been modified for human use. The Missouri is the largest reservoir system in the world, with six reservoirs in four states providing irrigation, flood control, and consistent water levels for navigation. Thirty-five percent of the river's length has been impounded and 32 percent has been channelized. The Corps of Engineers maintains a 9-foot-deep, 735-mile-long shipping channel between Sioux City, Iowa, and St. Louis. Levees now prevent flooding in bottomlands, 95 percent of which have been drained, cleared, and put into cropland. These alterations shortened the river by 72 miles! The Missouri in its natural meandering state was America's longest river, but now that it has been shortened, it is almost exactly the same length as the Mississippi. The sand and gravel mining, channelization, and pollution from the runoff from farms, factories, and cities threaten the health of this river. Japanese conservationist Tenaka Shozo said, "The care of rivers is not a matter of rivers, but of the human heart." Many hearts have turned to caring for the Missouri River. Groups like Missouri River Relief, the Missouri Watershed Information Network, the Coalition to Protect the Missouri River, and Friends of Big Muddy all work to keep the fish, wildlife, and people who depend on the river healthy and prosperous.

231.0 Down to Earth City

Exit 231 takes you to Earth City. The strange name comes from the fact that development started in 1971, shortly after the first Earth Day. The original plan for what now is known as Earth City Business Park included office buildings, industrial buildings, retail facilities, and 4,400 apartment units that combined would resemble a "city" with a daytime and nighttime population. A 2.7-mile-long dike was built high enough to turn back a 500-year flood. Millions of tons of earth were moved to protect Earth City.

ST. LOUIS, THE GATEWAY CITY

232.0 St. Louis County

As you crossed the river you entered into the highly urban county of St. Louis County. The junction of I-70 and I-270 is the busiest highway intersection in Missouri. Because of the busy traffic and difficulty seeing mile markers, we will present interesting things to see in the order that they appear and with the location given parenthetically.

Situated near the center of the United States, at the site where the two longest rivers in North America meet, St. Louis is not only a Gateway to the West, but a central location where barges, trains, planes, and automobiles intersect as they move people and freight across the country. In 1764, founder Pierre Laclede saw the potential of this strategic area and said that because of its "locality and central position" it "might become hereafter one of the finest cities in America." St. Louis's rich history includes tales of pioneers preparing to seek homes out west and immigrants finding homes here in what has become one of the finest cities.

The Gateway Arch will not come into view for another 15 miles. This is important information for those of you traveling with young children or overly inquisitive adults who will ask you repeatedly, "Can you see the Arch yet?" At the exact moment such excited travelers enter St. Louis they immediately hope to see the gleaming arch of silver rising above the horizon. You can reassure your anxious passengers that at mile 248 the perpetual silver rainbow will come into view.

Ahead you'll be able to see Lambert–St. Louis International Airport. St. Louis has been called "The City of Flight." In 2007, more than 15 million people passed through Lambert–St. Louis International Airport. Air travel here has a long history in St. Louis. Long before the Civil War, balloon pilots offered flights over the city. In 1911 an aviator enthralled crowds as he flew a seaplane up and down the river going under and over the Eads, Merchants, and McKinley bridges. In 1928, Lambert became the first municipally owned airport in the country. Many important aviation "firsts" happened at this site. Major Albert Lambert, whose first flight was with Orville Wright, opened a balloon launch station here in 1920. Other notable firsts here include the first experimental parachute jump in the world, the first airplane flight of a president (Theodore Roosevelt), and the first solo, nonstop flight across the Atlantic Ocean began here when Charles Lindbergh climbed into his *Spirit of St. Louis* and flew to New York to begin his historic journey. The McDonnell Aircraft

Company was founded here in 1939 and contributed more "firsts" for the United States—sending humans into space multiple times via the spacecrafts designed here. Since then, corporate headquarters and a manufacturing plant for McDonnell-Douglas, now part of the Boeing Company, have been located here. The large white buildings north of Lambert's runways are part of the Boeing complex. Boeing is the world's largest manufacturer of satellites, commercial jetliners, and military aircraft, and it is involved in the space shuttle and international space station programs. This location is part of their Integrated Defense Systems Military Aircraft and Missiles Systems Group. The Mercury spacecraft, built here, opened up new worlds of transportation on May 5, 1961, as it safely launched Alan Shepard, the first American into space. Alongside the airport on your left at mile 237 and then crossing over I-70 at 238.6 you can see the elevated rail lines of the MetroLink. Opened in 1993, this is the only light-rail system in Missouri. It makes about six trips per hour traveling at 55 mph. The MetroLink greatly benefits travelers, like you, on the highway. Their trains can carry 1,800 passengers per hour in a single direction, which means that about 1,600 cars per hour are removed from the highway in each direction. Almost 22 million people use MetroLink each year. You can travel for 46 miles on the MetroLink from Lambert Airport all the way into Illinois.

Ahead on the right you'll see many old houses and buildings of brick. In the Great Fire of 1849, most of St. Louis was destroyed after a steamboat caught fire, which spread to the highly flammable wooden warehouses on the shore and to the rest of the city. After the fire, most construction throughout the city was done with bricks rather than wood.

At 243 you begin driving on the Mark McGwire Highway, named for the St. Louis Cardinals homerun slugger. A 6-mile stretch of the highway honors McGwire for his record-breaking 70th homerun in the 1998 season, making it appropriate that it is honored by I-70. You'll get a glimpse of the Cardinals's stadium ahead to the right just before leaving Missouri.

Read about the ABB transformer factory on your right in the Westbound chapter (page 8). Just before mile 245 you'll see the Archer Daniels Midland (ADM) grain elevators on your left. ADM is the second-largest flour milling company in the United States. This particular mill, milling since 1913, produces 1,800,000 pounds of flour each day from soft wheat grown in Illinois and Missouri and from hard wheat grown in Kansas, Nebraska, and Oklahoma. The majority of their flour is sold in bulk to bakeries as far away as Texas and California. You might consume some of their flour from Pillsbury products and the breading on Tyson chicken patties (see their poultry partner at mile 79).

To the left as the road curves you can glimpse parts of the Bellefontaine cemetery. Bellefontaine includes the graves of explorer William Clark and many other famous people. Read more about this cemetery in the Westbound chapter (page 7).

The trees and lawn on the hill to the right are part of the 127-acre O'Fallon Park, formerly the estate of John O'Fallon. Col. John O'Fallon came to St. Louis after being wounded in the Battle of Tippecanoe in the War of 1812. He worked for his uncle William Clark of Lewis and Clark fame and built a fifty-room mansion on top of one of the Native American ceremonial mounds that gave St. Louis the nickname of Mound City.

Near mile 247, on the right side of the road in the distance, you will see a large white Corinthian-style pillar and a tall brick tower. The white pillar is the Grand water tower, built in 1871 in order to regulate the water from the city's first waterworks. The younger brick Bissell water tower was built in 1886. Both towers were put out of service in 1912. These interesting neighborhood landmarks are two of only seven historic water towers left in the United States.

At mile 247 you'll see your first glimpse of the tallest monument in the United States. Rising from the edge of the river 630 feet, twice as tall as the Statue of Liberty, the Gateway Arch inspires awe every time you enter the city. To some it means "I'm home," while to others it means a vacation or symbolizes the romanticism of the westward expansion of the United States. Since 1965, visitors have enjoyed taking the elevator to the top and also exploring the Museum of Westward Expansion below. To be included among the four million people that visit the Arch each year take Exit 250A on Memorial Drive. You can read

Grand water tower

more about this National Monument in the Westbound chapter (page 1).

If you can take your eyes off of the Arch for a moment (It's hard to do!), on your right you will see the two 215-foot-tall limestone spires of the Most Holy Trinity Catholic Church built

Most Holy Trinity Catholic
Church

in 1899 by German Catholics and modeled after the Strasburg Cathedral in Europe. Read more about this church in the Westbound chapter (page 6).

The Edward Jones Dome, completed in 1995, covers 14 acres. Up to 66,000 fans can fill the stadium to watch the St. Louis Rams play football. The 12.5-acre roof weighs more than 10 million pounds. The stadium contains enough concrete to make a 47-inch-wide sidewalk from St. Louis all the way back to Kansas City. In 1999 it was the site of the largest indoor gathering ever held in the United States, a mass celebrated by Pope John Paul II.

Across the highway from the Dome are the gas lamps and cobblestone streets of Laclede's Landing that have survived amid the paved highways and twentieth-century construction around them. The nineteenth-century warehouses in these nine blocks have been converted into trendy restaurants, clubs, and shops.

The exit for the Gateway Arch will also take you to the Basilica of St. Louis (on your left), or more lovingly called by locals, the "Old Cathedral." It is a survivor of the turbulent changes in St. Louis's history. Built in 1834, on the same site as the 1770 original Catholic church, it is one of the few buildings to survive the Great Fire of 1849 and then persevered as the only building left standing after forty blocks were torn down to make way for the grounds of the National Park Service's Jefferson National Expansion Memorial.

As you are heading up the ramp to the bridge to Illinois look quickly up the street to your right to glimpse the new Busch Stadium and home of the St. Louis Cardinals baseball team.

While crossing the Mississippi, look upriver to your left to see the ornate Eads Bridge. This National Historic Landmark is the oldest bridge across the Mississippi River. Railroad financiers in St. Louis raced to complete the construction in a rivalry against Chicago for the lead in railroad commerce. Self-taught engineer and ironclad boat builder James B. Eads used innovative construction techniques including many firsts to design St. Louis's first rail bridge. Eads did not give up, despite suffering a nervous breakdown while confronting many doubters and unprecedented engineering challenges. The double-deck, three-span bridge opened on July 4, 1874. It carried trains for 100 years until it was closed in 1974. Today the lower deck is used for the light-rail MetroLink commuter trains. The upper deck was opened for vehicular and pedestrian traffic on July 4, 2003.

FAREWELL

As you cross the grand and powerful Mississippi River, a river that St. Louis native poet T. S. Eliot called "a strong brown god," consider the words of John Kauffmann who wrote, "Rivers have what man most respects and longs for in his own life and thought—a capacity for renewal and replenishment, continual energy, creativity, cleansing." Our wish is that, like the Mississippi and all the rivers that you have crossed on your journey, you have found renewal and replenishment in the stories of the courage, resourcefulness, productivity, and enterprise of Missourians and inspiration in the beauty of Missouri's forests, fields, and streams. If you are continuing your journey east, we wish you smooth sailing and happy trails. Thank you for traveling with us across the Show Me State of Missouri.

References

The information presented in this book came from publications, websites, and interviews.

Many people provided us with information. We interviewed individuals along I-70 as well as people working in state agencies, particularly the Missouri Department of Transportation, Missouri Department of Conservation, and Missouri Department of Natural Resources. Some people volunteered information to us and provided us with directions, suggestions, and contact information.

Individuals whose names were supplied, and who provided us with helpful information, are listed below along with the publications and websites we used.

Publications

Axelrod, K., and B. Brumberg. *Watch It Made in the U.S.A.* Emeryville, Calif.: Avalon Travel Publishing, 2006.

Cable, T., and W. Maley. *Driving across Kansas: A Guide to I-70.* Lawrence: University Press of Kansas, 2003.

Canaday, B., and D. Niederer. "Looking for the Win-Win in Natural Resource Conservation: A Case History." *Proceedings 2003 Midwest Fish and Wildlife Meetings* (abstract).

Carlinsky, D. "A Lofty Past." *US Airways Attaché,* June 2004, 51–57.

Case, T. S. *Kansas City Review of Science and Industry* 5, no. 1 (May 1881): 23–24.

"Clydesdales Get New Home." *Kansas City Star,* November 28, 2008, A8.

Cooper, Brad. "Kansas Considers Guard Cables to Make Highways Safer." *Kansas City Star,* December 26, 2008. http://www.kansascity.com/115/story/953770.html, accessed December 27, 2008.

Curtis, C. H. *Why'd They Name It That?* Lake St. Louis, Mo.: Curtis Enterprises, 1992.

Darby, A. C. *"Show Me" Missouri.* Kansas City: Burton Publishing, 1938.

Davit, C. "Lowland Treasures." *Missouri Conservationist* 68, no. 8 (August 2007): 14–21.

Dickey, M. *Arrow Rock: Crossroads of the Missouri Frontier.* Arrow Rock, Mo.: Friends of Arrow Rock, 2004.

Earngey, B. *Missouri Roadsides: The Traveler's Companion.* Columbia: University of Missouri Press, 1995.

The Firefighters Memorial of Missouri [brochure]. Kingdom City: Foundation of Missouri, 2006.

Goodrich, J. W., and L. W. Gentzler. *Marking Missouri History.* Columbia: State Historical Society of Missouri, 1998.

Gregg, Josiah. *Commerce of the Prairies.* Norman: University of Oklahoma Press, 1954.

Hesse, A. K. *Little Germany on the Missouri.* Columbia: University of Missouri Press, 1998.

Kurz, D. *Shrubs and Woody Vines of Missouri.* Jefferson City: Conservation Commission of the State of Missouri, 1997.

———. *Trees of Missouri.* Jefferson City: Conservation Commission of the State of Missouri, 2003.

Lauk, S. "The Mystery of Missouri's Lettered Routes Unscrambled." *St. Joseph News-Press,* July 4, 2005, A1–A2.

Mason, T. "Private Pond Stocking." *Missouri Conservationist* 68, no. 5 (May 2007): 14–18.

Massey, D. *Insiders' Guide to St. Louis.* 2d ed. Guilford, Conn.: Morris Book Publishing, 2005.

McMillen, M. Ford. *A to Z Missouri: Dictionary of Missouri Place Names.* Columbia, Mo.: Pebble Publishing, 1996.

McNulty, E. *St. Louis Then and Now.* San Diego: Thunder Bay Press, 2000.

Missouri Department of Conservation. *Public Prairies of Missouri.* 4th ed. Jefferson City: Missouri Conservation Commission, 2003.

Moulton, G. E., ed. *The Journals of the Lewis & Clark Expedition.* Vol. 2, August 30, 1803–August 24, 1804. Lincoln: University of Nebraska Press, 1999.

Murphy, K. "First Lines of Defense." *Kansas City Star,* August 26, 2005, A1, A8.

Nagel, P. C. *Missouri—A History.* Lawrence: University Press of Kansas, 1977.

Nelson, P. W. *The Terrestrial Natural Communities of Missouri.* Jefferson City: Missouri Natural Areas Committee, 2005.

Painter, A., and I. Dilliard. *"I'm from Missouri!" Where Man and Mule Shaped the Heart of a Nation.* New York: Hastings House, 1951.

Palmer, B. *Missouri Forests: Their History, Values, and Management.* Jefferson City: Missouri Department of Conservation, 1991.

Plamondon, M. *Lewis and Clark Trail Maps: A Cartographic Reconstruction.* Vol. 1. Pullman: Washington State University Press, 2000.

United States Department of Interior. National Park Service. Missouri National Recreational River [brochure]. Washington, D.C.: U.S. Government Printing Office, 2003.

Unklesbay, A. G., and J. D. Vineyard. *Missouri Geology: 3 Billion Years of Volcanoes, Seas, Sediments, and Erosion.* Columbia: University of Missouri Press, 1992.

Interviews

The following individuals provided information about people and places included in this book.

John Aleksick, Boeing Company, St. Charles
Bill Auchley, resident, Montgomery City
Cassy Banks, resident, Sweet Springs
Brad Barlow, I-70 Speedway, Odessa
Tina Bender, Thurmond Stout, Inc., Higginsville
Scott Brooks, ADM Co., St. Louis
Patti Campbell, president, Cooper County Youth Fair, Boonville
Dr. David Clapsaddle, historian, Larned (KS)
Mike Cleary, AmerenUE Callaway Power Plant, Fulton
Cyndi Cogbill, Missouri Department of Natural Resources, Joplin
John Didion, Didion & Sons, Inc., St. Peters
Donald Dittmer, president, Concordia Area Heritage Society, Concordia
Sherry Fischer, Missouri Department of Conservation, Jefferson City
Mike Fraser, Missouri Department of Conservation, Kansas City
Marian Goodding, Missouri Department of Natural Resources, Brookfield
Don Griesenauer, Laborers AGC, High Hill
John Payne Harrison, Callaway Livestock Center, Kingdom City
Donna Howard, Florissant Sod Company, O'Fallon
Susan Jenkins, resident, Sweet Springs
Don Jones, Laborers AGC, High Hill
Elaine Margaret Justus, Missouri Department of Transportation, St. Joseph
Bill Lemmons, principal, St. Paul Lutheran High School, Concordia
Grady Manus, Daniel Boone Home and Boonesfield Village, Defiance
David L. Marshall, resident, Blacksburg (VA)
Dr. Maryellen H. McVicker, historian, Boonville
Lonnie Messbarger, Missouri Department of Conservation, St. Joseph
Marjorie Miller, Montgomery County Historical Society, Montgomery City
Dennis Mitmeir, resident, Higginsville
Richard Mucha, ABB, Inc., St. Louis
Elizabeth Murphy, Missouri Department of Natural Resources, Montgomery City
Tom Nagel, Missouri Department of Conservation, St. Joseph
Jackie Nierman, Greif Packaging LLC, Wright City
Glen Older, retired truck driver, St. Joseph
Mike Perry, Missouri Department of Conservation, St. Joseph
Roscoe Righter, director, Parks and Recreation, City of Blue Springs
Scott Ryan, Missouri Department of Conservation, St. Joseph
Cathie Schoppenhorst, Daniel Boone Home and Boonesfield Village, Defiance
Jerry Smith, St. Charles County Parks and Recreation Department, St. Charles

Jim Strodtman, resident, Wellington

Richard Tinsley, Tinsley Amusements, Inc., High Hill

Les Turelli, Meramec Caverns, Stanton

John Wade, resident, Higginsville

Bo Wendleton, vice president, Cooper County Fair, Boonville

Terry White, White Industries, Bates City

Ron and Lisa Williams, farmers, Odessa

Dick Wilson, Fire Fighters Memorial of Missouri, Fulton

Dr. Kristin E. S. Zapalac, Missouri Department of Natural Resources, St. Louis

Web Sources

ameren.com (Callaway and Sioux power plants)

atmizzou.missouri.edu (Mizzou Alumni Association)

ballparkdigest.com

bdhhfamily.com (Benjamin Cooper)

boeing.com

boonecountyfairgrounds.com

brainyencyclopedia.com (Marquis de La Fayette)

brownandcrouppen.com (Warren County)

btcomm.com/creek/road.htm

callaway.county.missouri.org

callawayfarms.com (Shryocks Callaway Farms)

catscale.com (Certified scales)

centralmethodist.edu

chambercommerce.com (Missouri Chamber of Commerce Directory)

corncobpipe.com (Missouri Meerschaum Company)

danville.www2.50megs.com/PEOPLEOFDANVILLE.htm (People of Danville)

dnr.mo.gov (Missouri Department of Natural Resources)

doerun.com (Doe Run Company)

dor.mo.gov (Missouri Department of Revenue)

earlyaviators.com

earthcityld.com (Earth City)

epa.gov

ericrogers.org (Nickerson Farms)

explorestlouis.com (St. Louis Convention and Visitors Commission)

flykci.com (Kansas City Airport)

gatewaynmra.org (Gateway Division NMRA)

Hannibal.net (*Hannibal Courier-Post*)

harley-davidson.com (Harley-Davidson Company)

historiclexington.com (Lexington Chamber of Commerce)

hsrc.org (Hazardous Substance Research Centers)

jchs.org (Jackson County)

kansascity.com (*Kansas City Star*)

kc.library.org (Kansas City Public Library)
kcgolddome.org (Cathedral of the Immaculate Conception)
kcmo.org (Kansas City)
keepsmilin.com (Meerschaum)
latimes.com
lewisandclarktrail.com
lyndonirwin.com (Lyndon Irwin Genealogy Page)
mdc.mo.gov (Missouri Department of Conservation)
migratorybirds.fws.gov/issues/towers/ (impacts of towers on bird mortality)
missouri.edu (University of Missouri)
mocorn.org (Missouri Corn Growers Association)
modot.mo.gov (Missouri Department of Transportation)
modot.org (Missouri railroads)
mopork.com (Missouri Pork Association)
mo-river.net (Mo-River-Net)
moriver.og (Missouri River Communities Network)
mostateparks.com (Missouri State Parks)
nass.usda.com (National Agriculture Statistics Service)
ncga.com (National Corn Growers Association)
netstate.com
oaaa.org (Outdoor Advertising Association of America)
odessamochamber.com (Chamber of Commerce, Odessa)
odessapuddlejumperdays.org (Odessa Puddle Jumper Days)
ofallon.mo.us
porlier.biz (Porlier Outdoor Advertising Company)
riverfronttimes.com (*Riverfront Times*)
route40.net (U.S. 40)
rvamerica.com
santafetrail.org
saskschools.ca (Early Days/The Homesteaders)
sciengineering.com (Repeater Station)
skyscraperpage.com (Skyscraper Source Media)
sos.mo.gov (Missouri Secretary of State)
splhs.org (St. Paul Lutheran High School)
stlouis.missouri.org (City of St. Louis Community Information Network)
stlouisrams.com
stltoday.com (*St. Louis Post–Dispatch*)
stpetersmo.net
thelibrary.springfield.missouri.org (Cooper County)
thelibrary.springfield.missouri.org (Springfield–Greene County Library)
towerill.com (website maintained by Old Birds, Inc.)
two-lane.com (*Two-Lane Roads Quarterly*)
westminster-mo.edu (Westminster College)

Index